OWL HOOT TRAIL

Publisher: Cathriona Tobin | Authors: Clinton R. Nixon and Kevin Kulp Layout: Michael Chaney | Art Direction: Beth Lewis | Artwork: Rich Longmore | Special thanks to Matthew Breen for proofreading and brilliant suggestions

TABLE OF CONTENTS

TABLE OF CONTENTS

PART ONE
RULES AND CHARACTER CREATION

CHAPTER ONE
HOW TO PLAY

Owl Hoot Trail is a role-playing game set in a fantasy version of the American Wild West. If you have played other fantasy roleplaying games, many things about this game will seem familiar.

In this game, the players act out the roles of interesting people in the game world. You might play a rough-ridin' cowboy, a fancy man or lady, a no-good horse thief, a steely-eyed marshal, or a mysterious mentalist.

One person playing this game must be the Game Master (GM). Everyone else is a player who controls one player character (PC) in the game. The GM controls all other characters and the environment.

THE GM'S JOB

The GM's job is to prepare and run adventures. You are going to be in charge of everything that goes on in the game world. That doesn't mean that you have to plan out everything happening before you can play. It does mean that you have to have an idea about what the game world is like, some specific places and people within it, and how they will react to the PCs. There're many ways to prepare an adventure and many resources on the Internet to help you. Here it is in a nutshell.

Make up situations. Think up some situations where two people or groups of people want something at odds with each other. Here are some examples.

* Some greedy gold miners want to run off a native tribe.
* A vampire lord is wanted by the law ... undead or alive!
* An iron dragon lives at the top of a mountain pass and eats anyone who tries to cross.

See the *Running the Game* section for more ideas and help creating situations.

Set up the adventure. Given a situation you've thought up, come up with the creatures and people involved. Write out game statistics for them and think about how they talk and act and react. Imagine the areas involved and sketch out some maps. Then, when the game starts, describe this to the players. You should decide where the PCs are at the beginning of the adventure.

Give the players hell. You will act out everybody and everything the PCs meet. Some will be friendly and that is part of the fun of the game. Some will not be friendly and that is also part of the fun. For a lot of people, that's the most fun. Don't pull punches. Have sneaky monsters who plan as well as the PCs do. Have dangerous environments full of pitfalls. Put the PCs in danger.

Reward the players. The players should be rewarding for thinking up clever solutions. You may well give them a situation they can't just shoot their way out of, and they should be rewarded in the game by thinking up a smart way out of it. You will also distribute experience points (XP) and treasure.

THE PLAYERS' JOB

As a player, you will have one character you control. Your job is to create that character at the beginning of the game and then decide what they do in the game. Your job is more self-explanatory than the GM's, but here are some things you should do.

Slay monsters and save the helpless. Your character isn't required to be a good person or a hero. With that said, it's assumed that when the chips are down, you will fight on the side of good for whatever reason you may have.

Work together. Your character might be a cold son-of-a-bitch, but remember that they are a character in a rough world and you are playing a game with friends. In the game world, the PCs might have arguments, but in the end they are a band of travelers with common goals.

Help the GM. The GM is in charge of the world, but you can help them out. First, play in their adventure. Don't go charging off into the brush when it's obvious they've made an adventure that goes into a mine. Second, let them know the kind of stuff you want to see in the game.

Be excited. You shouldn't hog the spotlight, but when it's time for your character to do something, do something cool. Be smart and keep your character from buying the farm, but don't cringe away from all danger. Describe what your character is doing with some detail. "I draw my Winston .45 and shoot the goblin in the shoulder" is more interesting than "I shoot him."

CHAPTER TWO

CHARACTER CREATION

The first thing a player needs to do to get ready for play is create a character. Creating a character is easy in *Owl Hoot Trail*. Get a character sheet by photocopying the one in the back of the book or printing the one on our website. Then, follow the instructions below.

HOW TO MAKE A CHARACTER

CHOOSE A RACE

Read the *Character Races* section (page 10) and then choose a race for your character. Record the race and any special racial benefits your character has.

CHOOSE AN ORIGIN

Is your character a *greenhorn* or a *native*?

* A greenhorn character grew up in civilization and is usually a new arrival to the frontier. They add +1 to their Learning skill.

* A native character grew up on the frontier, either in a tiny settlement or in a tribe that lives in the wild but trades in town. Tribes are of a single race, but it can be any race. Some tribes get by with greenhorns alright and some don't, and it's not easy for a greenhorn to tell

which are which. Native characters add +1 to their Wilderness skill.

Record the skill bonus from the origin you chose.

CHOOSE A CLASS

Read the *Character Classes* section (page 11) and then choose a class from your character. If you choose a gadgeteer, mentalist, preacher, or shaman, read the *Powers* section (page 23). Note any ability score restrictions your class has. You'll have to fulfil those in the next step. Some races tend towards certain classes, but you can choose any class you want.

CHOOSE YOUR ABILITY SCORES

Your character has 3 *ability scores*.

* **GRIT:** You got to be rough and tough.
* **DRAW:** You got to be quick and ready.
* **WITS:** You got to be awake and sharp.

All these abilities start at zero, plus any modifiers from your character's race. You have three points to split between these abilities. If you want, you can subtract 1 point from any ability, dropping it to -1, to add a point to another ability. You can only do this once.

Make sure that you allocate points in such a way that you meet your class-based ability score restrictions.

WRITE DOWN YOUR LEVEL

Write down 1 for your character's level and 0 for their experience points.

RECORD YOUR SKILLS

There are 5 skills: *Amity*, *Learning*, *Toughness*, *Wile*, and *Wilderness (page 18)*. Your character's skill bonus in each of them is equal to their level plus any bonus due to their class, origin or race. Record this and read the *Skills* section to learn more about how to use them.

CHOOSE YOUR POWERS

If you are playing a gadgeteer, mentalist, preacher, or shaman, choose a number of 1st-rank powers equal to your WITS. Pick one of these to be your character's *signature power*.

RECORD YOUR HIT POINTS

Your character starts with 10 + their GRIT score in *hit points (HP)*.

FIGURE OUT ATTACK, DEFENSE, AND INITIATIVE

Your character has an attack bonus for each type of attack. Write down their totals.

* *Melee attack bonus* = GRIT + level
* *Missile attack bonus* = DRAW + level
* *Power attack bonus* = WITS + level

Your character has a *Defense score* which indicates how hard they are to hit, and a *Mental Defense score* which indicates how hard it is for the supernatural to influence their mind.

* *Defense score (Def)* = 10 + DRAW + level
* *Mental Defense score (MDef)* = 10 + WITS + level

Your character may have some modifications to these scores based off their class. Record these at this time.

Initiative (init) determines the order of actions during combat and is rolled with a d6. Your character's *initiative bonus* is equal to their DRAW. Note this on your sheet.

PICK EQUIPMENT

Your character starts with $100 (or $150 if they're human) to spend on equipment. See the *Equipment* section (page 33) to choose what your character will start with.

HARDENED CHARACTERS

Owl Hoot Trail can be a dangerous place, and Boot Hill is full of people who forgot that bullets kill. If the GM wants player characters to have a little more longevity, increase their starting hit points from 10 + GRIT to 15 + GRIT. This bonus of +5 HP stays with characters as they advance. NPCs and monsters are not usually hardened.

RECORD YOUR WEAPONS

Record the weapons you chose for your character, and other weapons they are likely to use, such as an improvised weapon or fists. Beside each of these, write down their combat information, including your character's attack bonus with them and their damage bonus. Note that you should add your character's GRIT to any melee weapon damage.

FINISHING

If you haven't yet done so, name your character. Write down their characteristics, such as their age, hair and eye color, and distinctive scars. Your character is complete.

CHARACTER RACES

HALF'INS

There's a whole passel of *half'ins* out on the frontier. Half'ins are short, about 3 and a half feet on average and tend to be a little tubby. They like a good meal and a cold beer. Most are real friendly, but they're close-knit and don't take kindly to outsiders trying to take advantage of them.

Half'ins tend to be ruffians, scoundrels, scouts, mentalists, preachers, or shamans.

They get +1 to DRAW and a +1 to Amity. They also get a +1 to their Defense score for being so small.

HILL FOLK

Hill folk, or dwarves, are damn good miners and even better brewers. They're about 4 feet tall and almost always have large beards. They live in their own settlements in the hills and have their own government. Their women-folk don't come down from the hills and their towns are built like forts.

Hill folk get along with humans alright, though. They do a lot of trading and enjoy a lot of the same things humans do. They are very literal-minded, but enjoy a straight-forward joke.

Hill folk tend to be gunslingers, marshals (legally, they're marshals in their own settlements, not in human settlements), ruffians, scouts, gadgeteers, or preachers.

They get +1 to GRIT and a +1 to Toughness. Hill folk are also better at spotting underground traps and dangers. They gain a +3 bonus on any skill checks to spot such hazards.

HUMANS

Most folks are *humans*. Humans come in all shapes and sizes and can do what they want in life. They run the government, most shops and establishments, and there are plenty of native human tribes. Humans can be as nice as pie or wicked as midnight.

Humans get +1 to all skills. They also start with an extra $50. They can be any class they want.

ORCS

Orcs and humans have had their differences, but sometimes you got to live and let live. For the most part, humans and orcs rub elbows in the same places.

Greenskins are like any other type of people. There're good ones and bad ones. To hear it told, the bad ones are real bad, and there's truth to it. Orcs are stronger than humans, and an angry one will tear you apart. Then again, humans aren't blameless. Big green people with fangs and tusks look scary as hell, and some humans value an appearance over actions.

One thing you can say for certain about an orc: they won't cheat you. They don't lie – and that's a source of trouble a mile wide – and even the meanest one's got enough of a sense of honor to let a man die with a weapon in his hand. Those traditions run deep, and orcish tribes have an unpleasant custom of hunting down and publicly executing any dishonest orc who runs across their path.

Orcs tend to be gunslingers, ruffians, scouts, gadgeteers, or shamans. They can be marshals, but it's rare except in the most enlightened places.

They get +1 to GRIT and +1 to Toughness. They suffer a -2 penalty to Wile. In exchange, orcs are damn tough; orcs are *Hardy 1*. That means that injury rolls on an orc are always at -1 on the 2d6. In addition, orcs count every 2 days as 3 for the purpose of healing injuries.

SHEE

Shee, or elves, look like lean, rawboned humans with sunken cheeks and pointed ears. No one remembers a time that shee didn't live out West, and the greenhorn shee you meet are ones who moved to the city ages ago. Most native shee live in the wild but trade in town. They can make a baby with humans, but it ends up just being a real good-looking human. Shee are particularly clever, and are known for their deadly accuracy with a bow.

They tend to be scouts, gunslingers, ruffians, scoundrels, mentalists, or shamans.

They get +1 to WITS and a +1 to Wilderness. Shee also get a +1 to their missile attack bonus with any bow.

CHARACTER CLASSES

GUNSLINGER

Gunslingers solve most disputes with bullets. They gain a +2 bonus to Toughness and a +1 to Wile. They get a +1 bonus to all damage rolls with guns if they have a DRAW of 1 or more. This damage bonus increases by +1 at 3rd level and every 3 levels on. A gunslinger with a GRIT of 1 or more can hold a pistol in each hand and attack with both in the same combat round if they take a -2 on each attack roll.

Gunslingers use 1-handed melee weapons and any gun that's still got a bullet left. They usually need at least a 1 in DRAW to be effective, and 1 or more in GRIT if they want to fight two-handed.

MARSHAL

Marshals get a tin star and a license to keep order. They have a +1 bonus to Toughness and +2 to Amity. They don't get sick and get a +1 bonus to all defenses. This increases by +1 at 3rd level and every 3 levels on. Marshals with a WITS of 1 or more can detect if a soul's up to no good within 60' at will. Marshals with a GRIT of 1 or more can heal a body up to 2 hit points per level per day by sharing a drink.

A marshal can use any weapon, but gains a +1 bonus to missile attacks when using a firearm.

A character must be law-abiding to be a marshal. Most marshals have at least a 1 in GRIT and in WITS besides in order to use all their abilities.

RUFFIAN

Ruffians have a notoriously bad temper and can fight with just about anything they can get their hands on. They gain a +3 bonus to Toughness. A ruffian can be enraged once per day, which adds 3 to GRIT but subtracts 3 from WITS, lasting 1 round/ level.

Ruffians with a DRAW of 1 or higher are nimble enough to have a special *dirty fighting* melee attack. It does 1d6 + GRIT damage, increasing by one die type at 3rd level and every 3 levels on (that is, 1d8 at 3rd level, 1d10 at 6th, and 1d12 at 9th.) They can use this attack unarmed or with any improvised weapon they can put their hands on.

Ruffians can use all weapons. Most ruffians have a high GRIT to be better at melee combat, and have a 1 or more in DRAW in order to fight dirty.

SCOUNDREL

Scoundrels are no-good cheats and backstabbers. They have a +3 bonus to Wile. If they have a WITS score of 1 or more, scoundrels who successfully sneak up on a foe (usually Wile + DRAW, but depends on situation) can add their Wile skill rank to the damage of their first attack. Scoundrels can use their DRAW + level as their melee attack bonus instead of GRIT + level if they are using a 1-handed weapon.

A scoundrel can use any melee weapon except a sword, as that's a gentleman's weapon. They can use pistols and shotguns.

Most scoundrels are fast and agile, so consider putting 1 or more in DRAW. Put 1 or more in WITS to be able to backstab.

SCOUT

Scouts make their home wherever they may roam. They gain a +3 bonus to Wilderness and a +1 bonus to missile attacks at range 3 and above. At third level a scout with a GRIT of 1 or more may find themselves a wild animal to tame and be a loyal companion provided they are rough enough to tame it. This companion animal will improve along with the character, as explained in the *Advancement* chapter.

Scouts can use 1-handed melee weapons, bows, crossbows, and all firearms. A scout with a DRAW of 1 or more is agile enough to use two 1-handed melee weapons at the same time, making an attack with each if they take a -2 on each attack roll.

Scouts are notoriously tough and agile, so you may want to have 1 or better in GRIT and DRAW.

GADGETEER

Gadgeteers can make outlandish contraptions that can produce effects one might call magical. They get a +3 bonus to Learning. Their powers gain the *Brilliant Improvisation* ability, which gives them a bit more flexibility at the expense of burning out powers; see details in the Powers section below.

Gadgeteers use 1-handed melee weapons and crossbows. They can use one firearm type of their liking, chosen at character creation.

Most Gadgeteers work best when they're smart and nimble, so consider putting at least a 1 in WITS. A DRAW of 1 or more is likely to save the gadgeteer money when fixing burned out powers, as detailed in the Powers section later in these rules.

MENTALIST

Mentalists employ magics of a bewildering nature. They gain +3 bonus to Wile. A mentalist's tricks are of the enchanting, illusionary, and mind-affecting type.

They can use 1-handed weapons and pistols.

Strength of will matters to a mentalist. You'll probably want to have a 1 or better in WITS to be most effective. Mentalists with a DRAW of 1 or higher reduce damage caused by their spellcasting, as explained under the Powers section later in these rules.

PREACHER

Preachers tote the word of the All-Mighty the way others tote their shooters. They gain a +3 bonus to Amity. Their prayers have a miraculous effect, and their words can shame a wrong-doer into repenting.

In addition to spellcasting, preachers with a WITS of 1 or more also gain the ability to *Rebuke*. By quoting the Word of the All-Mighty, the Preacher can sap the will of wrongdoers. This is an at-will power attack vs MDef, 1d6 damage, range 0-1. A rebuke ignores physical cover but is language-dependent, and only works on creatures who can hear and understand the preacher's words. The GM is encouraged to add +1 damage when the rebuke is particularly well role-played.

A rebuke can reduce a creature to 0 HP but never results in a roll on the Injury table. Used against a cowpoke or cowpuncher, a 'taken out' result means the target surrenders, flees in fear to the nearest church to repent, or curls up on the floor wracked with guilt. Against a named character, note that an Amity or intimidation check to convince someone to surrender has a DC 5 lower against a foe with 0 HP.

CHARACTER CREATION EXAMPLE

Collin is creating a new 1st level character he's decided to name Cletus Sugarfoot.

He starts by choosing a race. He picks half'in. This gives him +1 to DRAW, +1 to Amity and +1 to Defense score for being so small.

He then chooses Origin. He figures Cletus grew up in a small half'in town out here in the West, spent his childhood outside and doesn't have any book learning. That makes him a native even though he didn't grow up in a tribe, giving him +1 to his Wilderness skill.

Now his class. Collin wants Cletus to be a gunslinger. That gives him +2 to Toughness and +1 to Wile. Depending on where he puts his ability scores, he'll get a +1 bonus to all damage rolls with guns and can fire two guns at once with a -2 penalty on each. He'll want at least a 1 in DRAW and a 1 in GRIT to be an effective gunslinger, but that's not going to be a problem.

Collin chooses Cletus' ability scores. He has +1 bonus in DRAW for being a half'in and 3 points to split between the 3 abilities. Collin wants the character to be fast and fight two-handed. He doesn't care much about WITS, so he puts 2 points in DRAW and chooses GRIT 1, DRAW 3, WITS 0. If he chose to, he could subtract 1 point from any ability to gain a point in another ability. Collin considers dropping to WITS -1 to gain DRAW 4, decides it's worth it, and settles on GRIT 1, DRAW 4, WITS -1.

Cletus starts with a skill bonus in each skill equal to his level, which is 1. Adding in bonuses from race, origin and class, Cletus' skills are Amity 2, Learning, 1, Toughness 3, Wilderness 2, and Wile 2.

Cletus isn't a gadgeteer, mentalist, preacher or shaman, so he has no powers. His hit points are normally equal to 10 + GRIT, so a flat 11. Collin asks if the GM is using the *Hardened Characters* option; she is, so Cletus' starting hit points are 16 instead.

The gunslinger's Melee attack bonus is GRIT + level, so +2. His Missile attack bonus is DRAW + level, so +5, and as a gunslinger Cletus could shoot two guns at +3/+3. His Power attack bonus is +0. Looking at defenses, Cletus has a Defense of 10 + DRAW + level, or Defense 16 with his half'in bonus. He's going to be hard to hit. Collin reminds himself to use cover or near total cover in gunfights for an extra +2 or +5 to his Defense. Cletus' Mental Defense score is much worse, only 10.

Collin has $100 to spend on equipment. He buys:

CHARACTER CREATION EXAMPLE (CONTINUED)

Backpack $5

Bedroll $1

Bandolier (holds 50 bullets) $5

Woolen Blanket $3

Boots $20

Clothes $25

Holster $3

Rope 50' $1

Waterskin $1

.32-cal ammo, box of 50 $5

Thames Arms Self-Cocking .32-cal revolver: 1d6 damage; range 0-1; 6 shot; $30.

This leaves Cletus with $0. He can't afford a second gun or a horse, so he resolves to shoot someone and steal both at the first opportunity.

Finally, Collin fills in his character's background. He decides Cletus Sugarfoot is from the notorious Sugarfoot Gang, on the run from the law and heading out to the frontier for new opportunities. Pale-eyed, short for his height at 3' tall and mean as a rattlesnake, he's got a grudge against bullies and is fast on the draw. Collin is ready to play.

Preachers are limited in their weapon use. There's a piece of scripture that Preachers take real serious, about how the shepherd hideth not his staff from the wolf. Preachers won't carry a weapon that can be easily concealed - no knives, no hatchets, no derringers, no pistols. Nothing stops a preacher from totin' a shotgun or a club, though, just so long as he isn't trying to hide it.

A preacher's going to be most happy with a minimum of 1 in WITS, which helps spellcasting and rebuking. A 1 or more in GRIT is useful if you expect to club varmints on a regular basis. GRIT also reduces damage caused by spellcasting, as explained in the Powers section later in these rules.

SHAMAN

Shamans talk to otherworldly spirits to protect the frontier. They gain a +3 bonus to Wilderness. Shamans can call on their spirits to perform mystic acts.

They use 1-handed melee weapons. They also use bows and crossbows and one firearm of choice.

Like preachers, shamans tend to be smart and hardy. Consider having at least a 1 in WITS to call spirits most effectively. A GRIT of 1 or more is likely to save the shaman money when regaining burned out powers, as detailed in the Powers section later in these rules.

CHAPTER THREE
ADVANCEMENT

EXPERIENCE POINTS

As characters go through adventures, they get better at the things they do. They earn *experience points* (XP) for their exploits. The Advancement Table on page 17 shows how many XP a character needs to get to a certain level.

GAINING EXPERIENCE POINTS

Characters gain experience points by having dangerous challenges. These challenges do not necessarily have to be physically dangerous. Quoting law to a judge in order to keep oneself out of jail is plenty dangerous, for example.

Whenever a character succeeds at an easy challenge, they gain 100 experience points. When they succeed at a moderately difficult challenge, they gain 200 experience points. When they succeed at a hard challenge, they gain 400 experience points. When they succeed at a deadly challenge, they gain 1000 experience points. When a character fails at any of the above, they get half that amount of XP.

An easy challenge is one where failure is unlikely, whether in a fight or when talking to someone important, but the result of the challenge is important to moving the adventure ahead.

A moderate challenge is one that uses up precious resources or time, but that the character has a fair chance of winning.

A hard challenge puts the character at real risk. They've still got a good chance, but it's not a fair fight any more. They could come out of this challenge losing a good deal of cash, pride, or skin.

A deadly challenge is what it sounds like. A body who takes on a deadly challenge usually has a chat with their Maker beforehand. A character in a deadly challenge has a real good chance of losing their life or their entire existence.

The amount of XP gained is up to the Game Master, who may choose amounts in between these three choices. The difficulty of a challenge may be determined after the challenge, when the GM can take stock of what happened. Experience is not split between characters: each character in a challenge gains the full amount of experience.

GAINING LEVELS

When your character has enough XP to gain a new level, consult the Advancement Table to see how many HP they now have. Your character will also increase all their skills, attack bonuses, and defenses. Depending on your character's class, they may gain other benefits.

Gunslingers get an +1 bonus to damage with guns at 1st, 3rd, 6th, and 9th levels so long as they have a DRAW of 1 or more.

Marshals get a +1 bonus to all defenses at 1st, 3rd, 6th, and 9th levels.

Ruffians have a special Dirty Fighting attack if they have a DRAW of 1 or more. It does 1d6 + GRIT damage at 1st level and increases to 1d8 + GRIT at 3rd, 1d10 + GRIT at 6th, and 1d12 + GRIT at 9th level.

Scoundrels gain an extra +1 bonus to Wile at 3rd, 6th, and 9th levels.

Scouts may find a wild animal to tame at 3rd level if they have a GRIT of 1 or more. They must tame it by themselves, although no skill check is required for this unless the GM prefers one. This animal, if its level is lower than the scout's, will gain a level every time the scout gains a level. In addition, this animal will gain +1 to its WITS at the scout's 6th and 9th levels.

Gadgeteers, mentalists, preachers, and shamans learn a new power automatically whenever they gain a level. This power must have a rank equal to or below 1/2 their new level rounded up.

ADVANCEMENT TABLE

Level	XP	HP
1st	0	GRIT + 10
2nd	2,000	GRIT + 14
3rd	5,000	GRIT + 18
4th	9,000	GRIT + 22
5th	14,000	GRIT + 26
6th	20,000	GRIT + 30
7th	27,000	GRIT + 33
8th	35,000	GRIT + 36
9th	45,000	GRIT + 38
10th	60,000	GRIT + 40

If using the Hardened Characters option, add +5 to all HP totals.

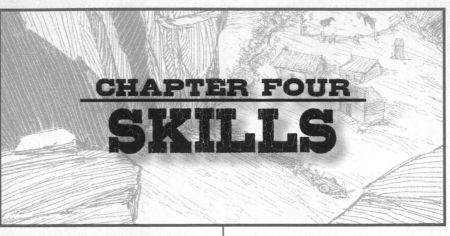

CHAPTER FOUR
SKILLS

SKILL RANKS AND TESTS

There are just 5 skills: Amity, Learning, Toughness, Wilderness, and Wile. Each of them has a *skill rank*.

* *Skill rank* = level + race bonus + class bonus

To test a skill, you must make a *skill roll* to beat a *Difficulty Class (DC)* determined by the GM.

* *Skill roll* = d20 + skill rank + whatever ability is most applicable + situation modifiers

DETERMINING DIFFICULTY CLASS

The Difficulty Class of a skill test can be determined from these rough guidelines.

* *Easy*: DC 10 (or no test at all most of the time)
* *Normal*: DC 15
* *Hard*: DC 20
* *Very Hard*: DC 25
* Add +5 for anything above that.

These are subjective. You can increase or decrease them in increments less than 5 if you like.

If two characters are competing, both players roll and then compare their totals to determine the winner.

AMITY

Hard looks and few words don't always work. Sometimes, you need to make friends. A smile and good cheer can help you get a good deal on that shotgun, get someone to spill the beans, or calm down a rough situation.

For example, guessing if someone may be lying or talking a soul into giving you the location of their employer who you plan to gun down would be Amity + WITS. Recovering from a faux pas in front of a fancy lady from Back East would be Amity + DRAW. Gathering up a band of loyal gunmen to back you up would be Amity + GRIT.

Amity checks to coax a foe into surrendering have a DC 5 lower than normal when the foe is on 0 HP.

LEARNING

An education can serve you well on the frontier. Someone's got to know the law, practice medicine, speak foreign languages, and the like.

For example, keeping your friend off the gallows by citing a technicality or a flaw in the charges no one else saw would use Learning + DRAW. Translating High Shee scratchings on an old cave wall would be Learning + WITS. Pulling a bullet out of a man's gut so he doesn't die would be Learning + GRIT.

TOUGHNESS

All sorts of things can test a body out on the frontier. There're cliffs to climb, deserts to cross, mind tricks to resist, and steers to wrestle.

For example, climbing would use Toughness + GRIT. Dodging a falling rock is Toughness + DRAW. Disbelieving a mirage in the hot desert would be Toughness + WITS. Breaking a persistent effect, such as trying to shock a friend out of a monster's mind control by burning them with a torch, is also a toughness + WITS check.

WILDERNESS

Learning will get you so far, but it doesn't prepare you for staying alive in the wilds. You need to know how to hunt a critter, what plants to eat, and how to get clean water.

For example, hunting down a wild boar would use Wilderness + DRAW. Recognizing something odd out in the wilderness or knowing how to treat a snakebite could use Wilderness + WITS. Crossing the plains half-dead on top of a horse with the blazing sun at your back would use Wilderness + GRIT.

WILE

A poker face can win you a lot more than the pot when you know how to use it. It can keep you out of the jailhouse or in someone's bed. Being a wily son-of-a-gun is a good way to sneak out the back of a saloon or behind a gunman.

For example, noticing something odd about a person or bluffing your way into winning a poker hand when all you've got is a pair of fives is Wile + WITS. Staring down an armed gunman and convincing them they don't want to open your box of trouble is Wile + GRIT. Sneaking up on a fellow would be Wile + DRAW, with a DC equal to the opponent's Mental Defense.

Intimidation checks (usually Wile + GRIT) to intimidate a foe into surrendering have a DC 5 lower than normal when the foe is on 0 HP.

OTHER

For unclear situations, roll a d20 + ability + level versus a DC; if no ability is applicable, roll d20 + level. If more than one skill might apply to a situation, generally select the one most beneficial for the player. Encourage players to be creative, particularly in combat; players may use skills the GM doesn't expect, such as bull-rushing a bandit off a cliff using Toughness + DRAW. If an unclear case crops up, quickly agree on the closest skill match and keep the game moving.

Skill	Examples of Use
Amity + GRIT	Gathering a posse, slowly earning a NPC's respect
Amity + DRAW	Quick-witted banter, making a good first impression
Amity + WITS	Noticing lies, being persuasive
Learning + GRIT	Medical knowledge and practice
Learning + DRAW	Quoting the law, recognizing clues
Learning + WITS	Translation, history, remembering obscure lore
Toughness + GRIT	Climbing, holding up under starvation or torture, blocking a foe from leaving a zone (opposed check)
Toughness + DRAW	Dodging, wrasslin' a steer, bull-rushing a foe into a different zone (opposed check)
Toughness + WITS	Disbelieving mirages, overcoming a persistent effect
Wilderness + GRIT	Crossing a barren desert
Wilderness + DRAW	Hunting a wild animal
Wilderness + WITS	Tracking people, noticing something odd in the wilderness
Wile + GRIT	Intimidation
Wile + DRAW	Most gambling, sneaking (base DC = foe's Mental Defense)
Wile + WITS	Bluffing, cheating when gambling, perception

ASSISTING WITH SKILL CHECKS

Characters can assist other characters in skill checks. One character (and usually no more than one unless the GM permits) can lend a hand. No roll for success is required so long as the player explains how he's helping. Both players roll a d20, and the assisted player can choose to use either result in his skill check. In combat, assisting another character takes an action.

An example: Collin's halfling gunslinger needs a hand climbing the outside wall of a bank. That's a toughness + GRIT check, and the GM decides it's a DC 12 to succeed. Tracey announces that her orcish ruffian is going to give the gunslinger a boost up, and both Collin and Tracey roll d20s. Collin chooses either to add to his +3 Toughness skill. He rolled a 4, Tracey rolled a 10, so he picks Tracey's and successfully climbs the bank's wall.

ADVANCED COMPETITION

Having two characters make skill rolls and comparing those rolls is simple and easy, but sometimes isn't real satisfying. Without a feeling of tension for the players involved, the competition may not feel like a struggle. In this case, the players involved should make the standard competitive skill roll. If the winning player's roll is not at least 15 points greater than the losing player's, then begin an extended contest. The players will roll again, and total their previous rolls with their current rolls. This will continue until one player's total is 15 or more points greater than the other player's roll, at which point the winning player has won the entire contest.

A duel should never feel boring, so advanced competitions often have a time limit. If the GM says "Advanced competition - victory threshold 15, round limit 5", then if nobody hits the 15 point target by the end of round 5, whoever's in the lead wins the contest.

During this contest, the two players should be describing the ups and downs of the rolls. If one can make a good case for changing the skill they are using for their roll, the GM should allow them to use a new skill for the next roll.

Advanced competitions can also be run with more than two characters. If every PC is chasing down one NPC, for instance, the GM rolls once for the NPC and each player rolls and tracks the results for their own character. Results are compared normally.

An example: Sheriff Tolbert is trying to run down Red Pete, a pickpocket. Tolbert's GRIT is 3 and Toughness is 5, for a total of 8. Pete's GRIT is 2 and Toughness is 3, for a total of 5. They roll and Pete gets lucky, rolling a 24 (5 + his dice roll of 19), while Tolbert rolls a total of 11 (8 + his dice roll of 3.) Pete takes off up the street and turns left into the horse stables. Tolbert's still on the shopkeep's porch and trips as he runs down the stairs, giving Pete the lead. They roll again and Tolbert rolls a 20, taking the total of his rolls to

31, while Pete rolls a 17, taking the total of his rolls to 41. Pete keeps the lead by diving into an alleyway, but Tolbert's gaining ground. Worried, Pete's player asks the GM if he can use his WITS of 3 + Wile of 6 for the next roll, saying he's going to hide in a dark corner and hope Tolbert passes him by. The GM says yes, and they roll again. Tolbert rolls a 24, bringing his total to 55, while Pete slips up and rolls a 13, bringing his total to 54. Tolbert sees through the ruse, and Pete's attempt to be tricky lost him valuable ground. In two more rolls, Tolbert's got Pete and is hauling him off to jail.

Note that 15 isn't a magic number. For a faster contest, the GM should choose 10, which would have solved the above example in one roll. For a slower one, the GM should choose 20, which would have made the above example last for one or two more rolls, likely enough.

ADVANCED COMPETITION AND GAMBLING

This system should be used for Gambling and card-playing when the GM wants to draw the challenge out. Be sure not to bore the other players with an extended contest that only one player is taking part in, however. Better to have most of the players participating, or to cut back to the gamblers periodically while other action is taking place.

An example: Boot Hill Bess, Bonesnap McGraw, and the Shee mentalist Four Good Aces are playing poker. Bess has a DRAW of 4, WITS of 0, and a +2 Wile. Bonesnap has a DRAW of 2, WITS of 1, and a Wile of +1. Four Good Aces has a DRAW of 1,

WITS of 4, and a Wile of +4. On the first round, all three characters agree on a starting ante - $5 - and pass a secret note to the GM saying whether they want to cheat or not. No one chooses to cheat the first round. Normal gambling is usually a Wile + DRAW check. Bess gets a 16 (6 + her die roll of 10), Bonesnap gets a 5 (3 + her dreadful roll of 2), and Aces gets a 20 (5 + her roll of 15.) Four Good Aces has now beaten Bonesnap's roll by 15, so Bonesnap folds and loses his $5 ante.

In the second round, Aces starts with 20 and Bess with 16. Aces raises the stakes by another $10; Bess stays in. They pass the GM a note to say whether they're cheating. Bess isn't, and rolls her gambling roll for a 17, bringing her total to 33. Aces does decide to cheat, so she'll be rolling Wile + WITS instead of Wile + DRAW. She rolls 21 (8 + her die roll of 13), bringing her total to 41. Bess is suspicious, and her player asks the GM "Is Aces cheating?" The GM tells her to roll Wile + WITS; Bess only gets a 13, lower than Aces's previous

roll of 21, so the GM tells Bess she didn't notice a thing. If the player hadn't asked, the GM wouldn't be obligated to ask for a Perception skill roll unless doing so would make the game more fun.

The third round of play has Aces cheating again after a $5 raise. Bess's roll totals a miserable 9, for a total of 42. Cheating, Aces rolls a 23 for a total of 64. With Aces's 64 beating Bess's total of 42 by more than 15 points, Four Good Aces wins. Once again Bess rolls her Wile + WITS to detect cheating, fails, and reluctantly crosses $20 off of her character sheet. Four Good Aces writes down an additional $25, smiles smugly, and saunters away.

This gambling system is flexible. So long as the players are having fun, it's simple to change how often bets are raised, and it may be preferable to run several quick contests instead of one longer competition. As always, things may change quickly if someone gets charmed or a character is caught cheating.

CHAPTER FIVE
POWERS

Gadgeteers, mentalists, preachers, and shamans all have lists of powers they can use. They learn a new power every level, and they start with a number equal to their WITS. They can learn and use any power on their list with a rank equal or below 1/2 their level rounded up.

DURING CHARACTER CREATION

Choose a set of 1st rank powers for your character's class equal to their WITS. Choose one of those powers as a *signature power* for your character. As your character gains new ranks of powers, you can choose one power at each rank as a new signature power.

MENTALISTS AND PREACHERS

For mentalists and preachers, using powers costs hit points. The cost is rolled randomly, using the Power Table below. This roll is made after the spell is cast and the HP are deducted then. If a character goes to 0 or less HP by using a power, they immediately pass out for 2d6 rounds but do not suffer an injury. Hit points lost due to using powers ignore temporary hit points and always come off of real hit points.

Mentalists subtract their DRAW from this damage; Preachers subtract their GRIT. As noted below, signature powers always do one less point of damage as well. Minimum damage is always 1 point.

An example: the shee mentalist Four Good Aces casts charm person, her signature spell. She rolls a 4 on her d4 damage. She subtracts her DRAW of 1, and 1 more point since it's a signature spell, and takes 2 points of damage. Her victim remarks how lovely that tiny trickle of blood from her nose looks in the moonlight.

GADGETEERS AND SHAMANS

Gadgeteers and shamans have to appease the whims of science and the spirit world. When they use a power, they have to make a *burnout roll*. They roll d20 + their level + their WITS. If they roll 12 + double the power rank or more, the power goes off immediately and they can use the power again later. If they roll less than 12 + double the power level, the power works but *burns out*. They temporarily lose the use of the power. A roll of 1 on the d20 is always a failure.

In order to get their powers back, a gadgeteer has got to recharge their batteries and a shaman has got to have a ritual to call their spirits. This recharging or ritual costs $5 times the level of power they are trying to recharge because of the metals or incense or whatever that they've got to get together. It takes a good 2 waking hours to recharge one power.

A gadgeteer who doesn't want to pay the recharge cost may make a DRAW + Level check at the same DC as the Burnout Roll; success means he was nimble enough to fix his gadget with existing supplies and does not need anything but time to fix that power. Likewise, shamans who succeed on a GRIT + level check do not need to spend money to recall their spirits.

An example: the shee shaman Five Dancing Hawks has burned out his minor flame spirit after failing the DC 14 WITS + level roll. It will take him a few hours to recall the flame spirit, but he would rather not spend $5 in supplies. Instead he rolls a GRIT + level check and makes a 15, higher than the DC 14. He recalls the spirit for free. As noted below, if Minor Flame Spirit was a signature power the DC for both rolls would only be DC 11.

If a gadgeteer has described his powers as emitting from a multi-purpose machine, the rest of the machine's powers are not affected if one or more powers burn out. Game mechanics shouldn't penalize a player's good descriptive flavor text of how they generate their powers.

A gadgeteer has the *Brilliant Improvisation* ability. They can spend a combat action to reconfigure a gadget for any lower-rank power, but it will immediately burn out the first time they use it. An improvised power can not be pushed. When doing normal post-burnout recharging, as described in the burnout rules above, the power returns to its normal function.

For instance, if the Gadgeteer urgently needs to get to the top of a wall, he can flip the polarity on the battery pack of his Electric Rifle, ionize the earth at the foot of the wall, and trigger the charge to repel himself skywards - reconfiguring his rank 3 Electric Rifle gadget for a rank 2 Magnolev Repulsifier gadget - but his Electric Rifle is going to be unusable until he can pull it apart and repair the damage later.

SIGNATURE POWERS

Characters can *push* their signature powers, trading the use of the power for greater effect. They can gain +5 on the power attack roll, or act as if they are one higher level when calculating the power's effect. For example, a 1st level gadgeteer with the signature power of *Deflector Coil* can have their force field work for 2 hours instead of 1 hour. You must decide to push the power before making any rolls.

Signature powers are easier than normal to cast. Gadgeteers and shamans subtract 3 from the usual Burnout DC when using a signature power. Mentalists and preachers lose one less hit point of damage per level of the signature power used, minimum of 1 hp damage.

Mentalists and preachers who push a power automatically take maximum HP cost from using the power. When gadgeteers and shamans push their powers, the power automatically burns out.

ATTACKING WITH POWERS

Any power that would affect another character requires a power attack roll. If it is a physical attack, like a flaming sphere or shaft of searing light, roll against the target's Defense score. If it is some other sort of attack, like putting someone to sleep or causing them to flee in fear, roll versus their Mental Defense score.

You do not have to roll if the effect is beneficial to the target. The target's player is the judge of this.

SPELLCASTING AND INCONSEQUENTIAL EFFECTS

When appropriate, all spellcasters are encouraged to describe their normal actions and skill checks as being the result of their magical powers. For instance, a mentalist making a normal Amity + DRAW skill check to make a good first impression on a saloon full of stranger may instead want to describe her successful roll as a direct result of her hypnotic powers. A shaman may announce that he made his Wilderness + DRAW check to hunt a wild animal because the spirits have shown him the correct trail. Minor details, such as a gadgeteer having a clockwork device to pour him drinks, are also fine as long as the GM doesn't think it is being over-used and there is no in-game mechanical effect.

DEFAULT ASSUMPTIONS ABOUT POWERS

The power descriptions are very short, so you may have to make some assumptions in order to use them. Unless otherwise stated, the target of a power must be within 1 zone of your character. The target of a power is usually 1 person, either your character or another character. When a power specifically targets multiple targets, a separate attack is rolled against each but damage is only rolled once and applies to all targets affected. A character is never considered their own ally for the purpose of a power.

GADGETEER POWERS

Gadgets are usually given colorful names by the gadgeteer. Sample names for powers are shown below.

1ST RANK GADGETS

Energon Projector: Range 0-1. 1d4+1 damage, no attack roll needed. For every 2 levels beyond 1st, the gadgeteer can create an additional blast, targeting the same or different targets.

Phosphorescence Agitator: Object shines like a lantern for 1 turn per level.

Horseless Freightwagon: Creates 3-foot-diameter horizontal disk that holds 100 pounds per level. Lasts for 1 hour per level and follows the gadgeteer.

Deflector Coil: Gives target +4 Defense bonus for 1 hour per level.

Crank-operated Electroprod: Touch delivers 1d6 per level electric shock damage (maximum of 5d6).

Vertical Decelerator: One object, person, or creature falls slowly for 1 round per level or until landing, taking no damage.

POWER TABLE

Level of Power	HP Cost	DC for Burnout Roll	Cost to Recharge
1	1d4	14	$5
2	2d4	16	$10
3	2d6	18	$15
4	2d8	20	$20
5	2d10	22	$25

2ND RANK GADGETS

Hydrochloric Torrent: Range 0-2. 2d4 damage for 1 round + 1 round per three levels. (2 rounds at 3rd level, 3 rounds at 6th, 4 rounds at 9th.)

Pyromatic Seeking-sphere: Creates rolling ball of fire, 2d6 damage, lasts 1 round per level. Gadgeteer can attack with ball each round.

Chameleon Field Emitter: Subject is invisible for 10 minutes per level or until it attacks.

Magnolev Repulsifier: Subject moves up and down 10 feet per round at gadgeteer's command for 1 minute/level. The maximum height of the target is 100 feet off the ground. This can also affect objects, as long as they're not much bigger than a mine cart.

Gecko-cling Adherence Suit: Grants the target the ability to walk on walls and ceilings for 10 minutes per level.

Automated Tumblelock: Opens one lock, door, or chest, even if locked by a power.

3RD RANK GADGETS

Pyromatic Explosion Projector: Range 1-3. 1d6 damage per level, attacks each target in one zone. Must roll power attack versus each creature in area.

Personal Ornithopter: Subject flies at running speed for 1 minute per level.

Handheld Nerve Disruptor: Range 0-3. Target is frozen in place and cannot even speak for 1 turn per level.

Electric Rifle: Range 0-3. Electricity deals 1d6 per level damage.

Luminoamplifier: Subject can see in the dark as if it were brightly lit for 10 minutes per level. Subject can also see invisible creatures and objects.

The Machine: Touch deals 1d6 damage per two levels; gadgeteer gains damage as temporary HP which last for 1 hour.

4TH RANK GADGETS

Etheric Sidestepper: Teleports the gadgeteer to any spot they can see.

Televisualizer: An invisible floating eye moves 30 feet per round for 1 minute per level. The gadgeteer can see through this eye.

Cryoprecipitation Inducer: Giant hail falls down over 2 zones for 1 round per level. 3d6 damage per round to all targets in the zone. Must roll power attack against all targets for the first round of effect. After that, any targets remaining in zone automatically take damage.

Motorized Entangulators: Tentacles grapple all within one zone for 1 round per level. Tentacles attack with gadgeteer's power attack score, do 1d6 + GRIT damage, and have GRIT equal to the gadgeteer's WITS. Creatures hit are treated as if hit by a lariat.

Glove-mounted Corrosion Coils: One ferrous object is instantly destroyed.

Clockwork Exoskeleton: The target ignores 10 points of damage per physical attack. Lasts for 1 turn per level or until 100 points of damage absorbed.

5TH RANK GADGETS

Difference Engine: Lets the gadgeteer ask one question and get cryptic but truthful answer.

Neurotoxic Fume Enfibulator: Poison cloud kills creatures of level 3 or less; causes an injury to others. Cloud fills two zones and lasts for 1 minute per level. The gadgeteer must make a power attack roll against every creature within the cloud or that enters the cloud each round. Once one injury is caused to a target, make no more attack rolls against it.

Neural Psi-Regresser: Subject's WITS score drops to -3 for 10 minutes per level.

Portable Hole Projector: Creates a passage through a wood or stone wall for 1 hour per level.

Sub-etheric Matter Displacer: Sends one willing target and all creatures touching the target up to 100 miles per level.

MENTALIST POWERS

COMMON MENTALIST TRICKS

All mentalists can perform these at will for 1 HP.

Dancing Lights: Creates lights for 1 minute.

Ghost Sound: Generate sounds for 1 round per level.

Prestidigitation: Perform minor sleight-of-hand tricks.

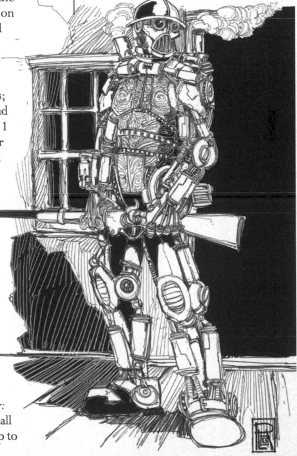

1ST RANK TRICKS

Charm Person: Makes one person a friend for 1 hour per level.

Disguise Self: Mentalist's appearance changes for 10 minutes per level.

Hypnotism: Fascinates 2d4 total levels of creatures for 1 round per level. Fascinated creatures can take no action unless attacked, which breaks the fascination.

Silent Illusion: Creates a minor illusion of mentalist's design while you concentrate.

Sleep: Puts 4 total levels of people or creatures into deep slumber for 1 minute per level.

Ventriloquism: Throws mentalist's voice for 1 minute per level.

2ND RANK TRICKS

ESP: Detect surface thoughts of anyone the mentalist can see and concentrate on for 10 minutes per level. The mentalist can change the target throughout the time period.

Hideous Laughter: Target can take no action for 1 round per level.

Hypnotic Pattern: Fascinates 2d4+level total levels of creatures for concentration plus 2 rounds.

Minor Illusion: As Silent Image plus some sound.

Mirror Image: Creates 1d4+1 ghostly decoys of the mentalist for

1 minute per level. Decoys vanish if successfully attacked.

Sixth Sense: Automatically sense danger and others' ill will toward the mentalist for 10 minutes per level. Gain +10 to Mental Defense to avoid being surprised.

3RD RANK TRICKS

Clairvoyance: Mentalist can see through the eyes of another living creature for 10 minutes per level.

Deep Slumber: Puts 10 total levels of creatures to sleep for 1 minute per level.

Halt: Person is frozen in place and cannot even speak without your permission for 10 minutes per level.

Major Illusion: As Minor Illusion, plus sound, smell, and thermal effects.

Suggestion: Compels subject to follow stated course of action for 1 hour per level or until completed.

4TH RANK TRICKS

Confusion: Subjects behave oddly for 1 round per level. Can affect all subjects within 2 zones.

Great Charm: Make one person or creature believe it is your ally for 1 day per level.

Invisible Killer: Dread spirit does 4d6 damage to subject.

Mind Travel: See and hear another area up to 1 mile away per level for 10 minutes per level.

Rainbow Pattern: Lights fascinate all

who see them for concentration plus 1 round per level.

5TH RANK TRICKS

Dominate Person: Control subject telepathically for 1 day per level. The mentalist does not need to stay within one zone of the subject to control them.

Persistent Illusion: As Major Illusion, but no concentration required; lasts for 1 minute per level.

Seeming: Changes appearance of 1 person per 2 levels for 12 hours.

Sending: Delivers short message to anyone anywhere, instantly.

Weaken Mind: Subject's WITS score drops to -4 for 1 day per level. At -4, humanoids cannot form sentences and talk with single-syllable words.

PREACHER POWERS

As noted in the class description, preachers can rebuke in addition to casting spells.

1ST RANK PRAYERS

Arise: One knocked out ally is immediately awakened.

Armor of God: Aura grants preacher +2 Defense bonus for 1 minute per level.

Bless: Present allies gain +1 on attack rolls and skill checks for 1 round per level.

Blessed Lead: Three bullets gain +1 on attack and damage. Lasts for 30 minutes or until discharged.

Divine Favor: The preacher gains +1 per three levels on attack and damage rolls for 1 minute.

Inspire: Gives 1d6+level temporary HP (maximum 1d6+5) to ally.

Light: Object shines like a lantern for 1 turn/level.

Purify Food and Drink: Purifies enough food and water for 2 people per level.

Rebuke Undead: One group of undead fears the preacher, staying in the shadows and refusing to attack.

2ND RANK PRAYERS

Aid: One ally gains +1 on all rolls, as well as 1d8+level temporary HP for 1 minute per level.

Choose Me: One attack targeting an ally targets the preacher instead. May be cast instantly after attack roll is made as a free action.

Delay Poison: Stops poison in system from harming subject for 1 hour per level.

Gentle Repose: Preserves one corpse from decay for 1 day per level.

Remove Paralysis: Frees one or more creatures from paralysis or slow effect.

Stop Bleeding: Halt the flow of blood from all of one body's wounds by touching them.

3RD RANK PRAYERS

Create Food and Water: Feeds three humans (or one horse) per level.

Prayer: All present allies get a +1 bonus on all rolls, all enemies take a −1 penalty for 1 round per level.

Remove Disease: Cures all diseases affecting subject.

Searing Light: Ray deals 1d8 damage per 2 levels, or 1d8 per level against undead. Attacks all targets in one zone.

Speak with Dead: One corpse answers one question per 2 levels.

Tongues: Speak any language for 10 minutes per level.

4TH RANK PRAYERS

Discern Lies: Reveals deliberate falsehoods for 1 minute per level or until concentration ends.

Freedom of Movement: Subject moves normally despite impediments for 10 minutes per level. Can move at full speed through mud, water, or any viscous substance, and is not slowed by wounds or bonds.

Heal: Heal one injury by touch.

Neutralize Poison: Immunizes subject against poison for 10 minutes per level, detoxifies venom in or on subject.

Sanctuary: The preacher and one willing target they are touching cannot be harmed by attacks for 1 turn per level. The preacher and the target must concentrate, allowing for no other actions beyond walking.

5TH RANK PRAYERS

Atonement: Removes burden of misdeeds from subject.

Commune: Deity answers one yes-or-no question per 2 levels.

Flame Strike: Smite foes with divine fire. 1d6 per level damage to 2 zones worth of foes.

Raise Dead: Restores life to subject who died no more than one day per level ago. Gentle Repose can double this time limit.

True Seeing: Lets you see all things as they really are for 1 minute per level.

Wrath of God: Cause an injury in one target. Target takes +1 on the injury roll.

SHAMAN POWERS

0 RANK SPIRITS

All shamans can perform this at will for 1 HP.

Spirit of the Hearth: Minor, inconsequential tasks. Repair a broken or torn object, cook a meal, sweep a floor.

1ST RANK SPIRITS

Beast-Talking Spirit: Shaman can communicate with animals for 1 minute per level.

Minor Flame Spirit: Range 0-1; 1d6 damage + 1 per level, touch or thrown.

Spirit Veil: Fog surrounds the shaman, providing concealment and partial cover for 1 minute per level.

Spirit of the Tangling Thorn: Plants entangle everyone within 2 zones for 1 minute per level. All movement within these zones is reduced to half normal movement, and it takes one full round to move within a zone and two full rounds to move from one zone into another.

Venom Spirit: Detect poison in one creature or object; become immune to poison for 1 round per level.

2ND RANK SPIRITS

Calm the Bestial Fury: Make one normal animal your friend for 1 hour per level.

Angering the Spirits of Iron: Makes metal so hot it damages those who touch it. Lasts 1 round per level. Does 1d6 damage on the first round, and gains 1d6 damage per round to a maximum of 4d6.

Curse of Vermin: Summons a swarm of bats, rats, or spiders for concentration plus 2 rounds. Swarm attacks all creatures in one zone for 1d6 damage, using the shaman's power bonus to attack.

Aspect of the Ancient Tree: The shaman looks exactly like a tree for 1 hour per level.

Twisting the Wood: Bends one solid piece of wood into any shape.

Spirit of Winds: Huge gust of wind blows away or knocks down smaller creatures.

3RD RANK SPIRITS

Call Forth the Dead Voice: Communicate with the dead. DC 10 + 1 per year dead. Dead may be hostile.

Spirit of the Bleeding Thorn: Plants entangle everyone within 2 zones for 1 hour per level, creatures in area automatically take 1d6 damage each round within area, and are slowed as with Plant Spirit.

River Carves the Stone: Sculpts one solid piece of stone into any shape.

Anger of the Storm: Range 1-4. Calls down 3d6 damage lightning bolts from the sky twice per round for 1 round per level. Bolts must target two different targets.

In the Water Spirit's Embrace: Subjects can breath under water for 2 hours per level divided by number of subjects.

Channelling the Warrior's Soul: Cause a weapon to do an extra 1d6 damage for 1 minute per level.

4TH RANK SPIRITS

By Spirits Borne Aloft: Subject treads on air for 1 turn per level.

Singing Forth the Corpse: Creates level x 2 total levels of undead skeletons or zombies from corpses. Undead obey simple commands.

Winter Spirit's Wrath: Hail does 5d6 damage to everything in 2 zones.

Reincarnate: Brings dead subject back in random body chosen by GM.

Spears of the Earth: Stone spikes lance from the ground, causing 2d8 damage to all creatures in 2 zones. Spikes are permanent and slow movement through area as with Plant Spirit. Movement through area automatically causes 1d8 damage per round.

5TH RANK SPIRITS

Awaken the Spirit Within: Animal or tree gains human intellect and the power of speech.

Wisdom of the Ancestors: You may ask ancient spirit 1 yes-or-no question per level. Spirit may not know all answers. Spirit may be cryptic. Takes 1 turn to use this power.

Fury of the Storm: As Anger of the Storm, but does 5d6 per bolt.

Unleashing the Spirits of Flame: Creates barrier of fire; deals 2d6 + level per round fire damage over two zones. Lasts 1 round per level.

Curse of the Locusts: 1d4+1 locust swarms attack creatures for 1 minute per level. Each swarm attacks foes for 2d6 + the shaman's WITS damage, using the shaman's power bonus to attack.

Spirit's Quest: Place a command on a creature to carry out a service. Creature must be able to understand you. Creature will not kill itself. Creature must follow instructions until quest is complete or take 2d6 damage per day and be unable to recover HP.

CHAPTER SIX
EQUIPMENT

The price of a piece of equipment varies wildly on the frontier, depending on quality, scarcity, the look on your face, and the drunkenness of the shopkeep. Any prices here are roughly fair and not likely to reflect prices in the game after you buy your character's initial equipment.

There's no way to list here on one page everything a character might need. My recommendation to you is to find an old 1890's Sears & Roebuck or Montgomery Ward catalog. They sell reproductions of these cheap. Take prices from there and multiply by 10.

DRY GOODS

* Backpack, $5.
* Bedroll, $1.
* Bandolier, holds 50 bullets, $5.
* Blanket, for a bed, $1.
* Blanket, woolen, big enough to use as a tarp or a tent, $3.
* Books on subjects such as accounting, botany, cooking, history, mechanics, or other sciences, $10-40.
* Boots, $20.
* Candles, box of 6, $0.20.
* Clothes, a set for walking around in, $25.
* Coat, leather, $50.

* Holster, $3.
* Holster, quick-draw-style (always win initiative ties), $6.
* Holy book, pocket-sized, $10.
* Holy book, gilt edged, fancy hardback, $85.
* Journal book, $5.
* Pack of cards, $5.
* Paper, 10 sheets, $4.
* Quilt, $25.
* Sack, small, $0.25.
* Sack, large, $1.50.
* Shoes, $12.
* Shoes, dress, $35.
* Suit, Sunday, $80.
* Suit, for a fancy-pants, $115.
* Tent, waterproof, $35.
* Waterskin, $1.

HARDWARE

* Bottle and cork, $2.
* Block and tackle, $12.
* Flask, $0.50.
* Hammer, small, $2.
* Holy water, 1 flask, $25.
* Ink, 1 oz., $8.

* Lantern, $10.
* Lock, $20.
* Lockpicks, $60.
* Manacles, $15.
* Mirror, hand, $5.
* Oil, 1 flask, $2.
* Padlock, $20.
* Pick, miner's, $3.
* Pole, 10 ft., $0.50.
* Rope, 50', $1.
* Spade or shovel, $2.
* Spikes, iron, 12, $2.
* Wolfsbane, fist full, $20.

TACK

* Bit and bridle, $10.
* Cart, ready to be pulled by an animal, $80.
* Hackamore, a type of animal headgear that does not require a bit, $8.
* Halter, $4.
* Saddle, $45 to $250.
* Saddlebags, $10.

FOOD AND SHELTER

* Pemmican (trail rations), 1 day's worth, $2.
* Unpreserved rations, 1 day's worth, $0.75.
* OK meal, $0.25.
* Fancy meal, $5 or more.
* Hotel room, 1 night, $10-100.
* Stabling and hay for a horse, donkey, or mule, $1 per night.

ANIMALS

Dog: You can find a dog that'll follow you around for the price of a slice of ham. If you want a well-trained dog, one that'll stand guard and protect a man, expect to shell out about $25.

Donkey: A donkey's a good beast of burden and can walk all day without tiring much. A donkey'll cost you between $15 for a run-down old jenny up to $100 for a tough jack. A breeding jack can cost up to $250.

Horse: You can get a no-good horse for as cheap at $20 if you know who to talk to. It won't ride worth a damn, though. If you want a horse you can ride cross-country all day, you'll pay $50 easy, $75 if you want one that has a lick of sense around cattle. A messenger horse, one that a mail boy would ride, running it hard all day, can cost $150 or $200. A lot of those boys work 3 or 4 years to pay off their horse. And, of course, a breeding horse can go for sums of money you've never seen before, $1000 or more. A no-good horse has a Toughness of +0, while an average horse has a Toughness of +5. A messenger horse could have a Toughness of +10, and the best of horses might have a Toughness of +15, but good luck trying to find someone who'll sell you one.

Mule: A mule can be as big as a horse, as stubborn as a donkey, and as smart as a dog. You can ride a mule, and some say it's smoother than a good horse, although a mule often as not thinks it's smarter than its rider. For packing and riding in mountains, though, a mule can't be beat. You won't find any cheap mules, but you won't find any too expensive, either. A mule will run you $40 for a smaller or more ornery one, up to $250 for a prize mule. A cheap mule will have a Toughness of +5 while an expensive one might have up to +10.

WEAPONS

MELEE WEAPONS

Punching or kicking: 1d3 damage; free as the day you were born.

Hunting knife or large pocket knife: 1d4 damage; $5.

Throwing knife: 1d4 damage; thrown range of 0; $6.

Bowie knife: 1d6 damage; $12.

Hatchet: 1d6 damage; thrown range of 0; $6.

Club or wooden beam: 1d4 damage; $1.

Walking staff: 1d4+1 damage; 2-handed; +1 to climbing or walking; $4.

Axe handle: 1d6 damage; 2-handed; $2.

Axe: 1d8 damage; 2-handed; $10.

Hammer, 4-pound: 1d4 damage; thrown range of 0; $4.

Hammer, 10-pound: 1d6+1 damage; 2-handed; $8. Requires GRIT of 1.

Saber or other one-handed sword: 1d8 damage; $75.

Widowmaker sword: 1d10 damage; 2-handed; $130.

Most improvised weapons: 1d4 damage.

BOWS

Hunting bow: 1d6 damage; range of 1-3; $25.

Long bow, shee-made: 1d6+GRIT damage; range of 1-4; $70. Requires GRIT of 1.

Crossbow: 1d6 damage; range of 1-4; takes 1 round to reload; $30.

Heavy crossbow: 2d4+2 damage; range of 1-4; takes 3 - GRIT rounds to reload, minimum of 1; $50.

GUNS

Yellow Jacket .22-cal revolver: 1d4+1 damage; range of 0; 7 shot, $10.

Hamilton Improved Double-Action .32-cal revolver: 1d6 damage; range of 0-1, 6 shot, $18. Known to explode on a roll of 1.

Thames Arms Self-Cocking .32-cal revolver: 1d6 damage; range 0-1; 6 shot; $30.

Mustang's Frontier Sliding Ejector .38-cal revolver: 1d6+1 damage; range 0-1; 5 shot, $35.

Mustang's Army Service Pistol .41-cal: Now available for sale to all! 2d4 damage; range 0-1; 6 shot; $65.

Surti & Sfinni Classic .45-cal revolver: Made by the hill folk. 2d6 damage; range 0-2; 5 shot; $130. Requires GRIT of 1. Lifetime guarantee.

Bulfinch & Hammersmith's "Foghorn" .50-cal revolver: 2d6+2 damage; range 0-2; 5 shot; $200. $25 extra for pearl stock. Requires GRIT of 2.

Blued finish on all the above $5 extra.

Mustang's Lightning Jr .22-cal rifle: 1d4+1 damage; range 2-3; 15 shot; $40.

Mustang's Lightning Rifles: Comes in .32, .38, and .45 calibers (1d6+2/1d6+3/2d6+2). Range 2-3; 15 shot; $70/85/140.

Wyvern Breech-Loading Shotgun: 3d6 at range 0; 2d4 at range 1; 1d6 at range 2; range of 0-1; single shot; $50.

Hellhound Shotgun: 3d6 at range 0, 2d6 at range 1, 1d6 at range 2; range of 0-1; 2 barrels; $120. Special order "Cerberus" 3-barrel edition; $250. Can fire all barrels at once, adding +1d6 damage per extra barrel.

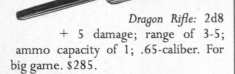

Dragon Rifle: 2d8 + 5 damage; range of 3-5; ammo capacity of 1; .65-caliber. For big game. $285.

OPTIONAL WEAPONS

Some weapons are more complicated, enough that the GM may wish to approve them first.

Black powder, dynamite and similar explosives:

Blowing things up is really the niche of the gadgeteer in *Owl Hoot Trail*, and it's recommended that explosives are best represented by a gadgeteer applying his powers - that is, explosives simply aren't an available option for those who aren't trained to use them. If you wish to make explosives available to all characters as a piece of equipment, use the following rules.

Explosives attack all targets in one zone when they go off. The attacker rolls power attack versus each creature in area; damage is rolled only once. Misses inflict half damage. Lighting an explosive's fuse requires the attacker to make a *Fuse Check*, a power attack against a specified DC; failure indicates a misjudged fuse, and the explosive immediately explodes in the thrower's zone instead of the target zone. Gadgeteers gain +2 on this check.

If an attacker wishes to delay the explosion by leaving a longer fuse, they may purposefully delay an explosion for 1-3 rounds. This does not affect their fuse check, which still must be made upon lighting the fuse.

Black Powder: Range 0-1; 3d6 damage; DC 13 fuse check to successfully throw. $25

Dynamite: Range 0-1; 5d6 damage; DC 15 fuse check to successfully throw. $50

Nitro: Range 0-1; 7d6 damage; DC 17 fuse check to successfully throw. Nitro is notoriously unstable, and requires a fuse check if dropped or sharply jostled. If this check is failed, the nitro explodes instantly. $100 when available

WEAPON RANGES

Missile weapons can fire one zone further than their stated range at -2 to attack, or one zone closer than their stated range at -5 to attack. For instance, a Yellow Jacket revolver is only good for close-up work, but a Mustang Lightning rifle is -5 to hit someone one zone away and unusable against a target in the same zone. Zones are explained under Fighting, later in the rules.

AMMUNITION

- .22-cal, box of 50, $5.
- .32-cal, box of 50, $10.
- .38-cal or .41-cal, box of 50, $15.
- .45-cal or .50-cal, box of 50, $22.
- .65-cal: box of 10. $10.

- Shotgun shells: a box of 20, $10. Can get standard buckshot or birdshot. Birdshot loses one in range, and does half damage, but has +5 to hit.
- Arrows and crossbow bolts, dozen, $3.

Gatling gun: Ranged attack against every creature in the target zone, dealing 2d6 damage; range 2-3; ammo capacity of 200 or more. Requires a round to deploy; also requires a combat action to reposition if the target zone changes. Requires two operators. $2000

A Gatling gun is extremely effective at holding a choke point from a prepared position. In close quarters, chaos, or ambush situations, it's a lot less useful than a six-gun - too many wasted actions setting it up, two characters are needed to operate it, ammunition costs mount up quickly, and by the time the gun is deployed the characters probably have allies in the target zone with their foes. Its range of 2-3 means that it can engage targets in an adjacent zone at a -5 penalty, and can't engage targets in the same zone. Since it is pulled around on wheels, it's not the most convenient weapon to transport across long distances or difficult terrain. That said, nothing is its equal for killing large numbers of enemies very, very quickly.

Special: when used by someone large like an ogre who can swing it around like an oversized shotgun, some of these limitations go away. Range becomes 1-3, no extra operator required, and no extra combat action is needed to switch target zones. A giant creature wielding a Gatling gun is typically trailin'.

Lariat (or Lasso): Range 0. A character must spend one combat action twirling a lariat, and a second combat action to throw it. On a successful ranged attack, the target is trailin' and cannot leave its zone. The target may free itself by using a combat action to successfully make a Normal (DC 15) GRIT + level or DRAW + level check (target's choice), +5 DC per additional lariat. If the same target is affected by two or more lariats at once, the only combat action they can take without GM approval is to try and escape.

Whip: 1d3 damage; 1-handed; $10. Uses DRAW + level to attack. Can knock things out of people's hands with an attack instead of doing damage. Can grab things if hit with a Hard (DC 20) Wile + DRAW test.

CHAPTER SEVEN
ADVENTURING

TIME AND MOVEMENT

When you need to track time in the game, you can use turns, which are equal to 10 minutes. These are used to measure movement and lingering effects from powers.

In one turn, a character can walk about 2000 feet. One turn out of every six should be spent resting in order to continue traveling at that speed, so characters can walk over clear land at about 2 miles per hour. It takes much longer to move through forest, over rocks, uphill, underground, or anywhere else where footing is unsure or visibility is not clear. The following list shows some example conditions and the rate at which characters can move per turn.

* Creeping quietly over rocks in a twisty cave: 100 feet

* Walking through a forest or brush: 400 feet

* Forced march: 3500 feet

* Running: 1 mile

* Being heavily encumbered: half speed

In eight hours of walking over clear land, a character should be able to travel 12-15 miles, depending on breaks. An eight-hour forced march over clear land would let a character travel 24-28 miles, and they will be exhausted. A forced march of that length would require at least a hard Toughness check.

Traveling by horse is much faster. A horse can usually travel 25-30 miles in a day without a problem. A horse can walk at 3-4 miles per hour (MPH), trot at 8-9 MPH, canter at about 15 MPH, and gallop at 35-40 MPH. In order to sustain a canter, the horse needs to make a Toughness check at 3 miles (DC 15) and each mile after that, adding 3 to the DC each time, i.e., DC 18 at 4 miles, DC 21 at 5 miles, and so on. In order to sustain a gallop, the horse needs to make a Toughness check at 1 mile (DC 15) and each mile after that, adding 5 to the DC each time, i.e., DC 20 at 2 miles, DC 25 at 3 miles, and so on. If the horse fails, it must begin to walk and must make a Toughness check at the same DC in order to move faster again. The DC goes down by 1 per turn of walking. You can force a horse to keep going after a failed roll with an Amity + GRIT check at the same DC, but the horse has to keep making Toughness checks. If it fails by 10, it collapses; if it fails by 15, it dies.

Traveling by mule is as fast as traveling by horse, but you aren't going to get a mule to canter more than 2 miles, or run more than half a mile, no way, no how.

HORSE CHASES

At some point, most people on the frontier find themselves on one end of a chase. If your character ends up in this situation, you will likely want some rules find out the result. The simplest method is to add your character's GRIT to their horse's Toughness and make a skill roll versus the other guy's GRIT + their horse's Toughness. Horse chases – or any chase for that matter – are a good time to try the advanced competition rules from the Skills chapter.

HAZARDS AND SITUATIONS

Characters will encounter many hazards and situations in their journeys. Here's a few.

Bleeding: Lose 1d6 GRIT per hour. If GRIT reaches -5, character dies. Severe bleeding may be 1d6 GRIT per turn or even per minute. GRIT returns at rate of 1/day. Bleeding can be stopped through prayers, cauterization, surgery or self-surgery.

Breaking a persistent effect: While Mental Defense (MDef) is a passive defense that protects a character from mental effects, roll a Toughness + WITS check to actively attempt to break a persistent effect that has a DC. For instance, a mentalist trying to charm your scoundrel targets your MDef. If your friend slaps you and throws a drink in your face to try and break the spell, roll a Toughness + WITS check against the original DC.

Cauterization: Roll Toughness + GRIT versus DC 20. Bleeding will stop regardless of success or failure. If roll is failed, lose one GRIT permanently and pass out.

Crawlin' through Hell: Occasionally a character finds herself parched and exhausted, staggering through inhospitable terrain with no water. A character must make Hard Toughness + GRIT checks, temporarily losing 1 point of GRIT and WITS with each failed check until getting some water and rest. The frequency of checks is up to the GM, with a usual minimum of 2 per day (and more for particularly difficult conditions). As noted below under Damage and Injury, reaching -5 GRIT results in death; -5 WITS results in catatonia or raving. Abilities lost in this way each typically return at a rate of 1/day of rest.

Disease: Standing water and certain monsters, such as Goliath Rats, often carry disease. Diseases can also be caught from other people who are ill. Diseases often reduce GRIT, DRAW, WITS or HP slowly over time until cured. Many preachers can cure disease, and a sawbones may occasionally be able to help as well. To avoid catching a disease, roll a successful Toughness + GRIT check at a GM-chosen DC after being exposed. Once cured, GRIT, DRAW and WITS each return at a rate of 1/week, or faster if the GM prefers.

Drowning: If a character is underwater and holding their breath, roll Toughness + GRIT every minute, starting at DC 10 and adding 5 at each check. If a check is failed, the character drowns and will die in 1 minute.

Extreme Heat & Cold: If not wearing suitable protection, roll Wilderness + GRIT every 10 minutes (DC 15, +1 per previous check), taking 1d6 damage on failed rolls. Appropriate clothing, shelter or precautions reduce the frequency of checks.

Falling: 1d6 damage per 10', half damage on a successful Toughness + DRAW roll. The DC is the depth fallen in feet.

Poison: Roll Wilderness + GRIT to avoid or for half, depending on poison. Effect varies with poison type.

Self-surgery: If a character has to remove a bullet from themselves after an injury, they'll need a knife, whiskey, and fire to cauterize the wound. Roll Learning + GRIT versus DC 20 to pull out the bullet. If failed, pass out for 1d6 turns and keep bleeding.

Spikes: add +1 point to falling damage per 10' fallen, max +10.

Surgery: If a character has to remove a bullet from someone else after an injury, they'll need a knife, whiskey, and fire to cauterize the wound. The character performing the surgery rolls Learning + GRIT versus DC 15 to pull out the bullet. If failed, the patient passes out for 1d6 turns and keeps bleeding.

Traps: Mines and other areas often have traps. If a character searches for a trap, they will spot it with a successful Wile + WITS check. Most traps require a Normal or Hard DC to spot. A spotted trap can often be avoided. If a character does something

which could trigger a trap, the trap goes off. A successful Toughness + DRAW check at a GM-chosen DC (usually Normal to Hard) usually reduces damage by half. Damage varies by trap but is often 1d6 per level.

CHANCE ENCOUNTERS

The players' characters will meet many other characters. The GM may have already determined how those characters feel about the PCs. If not, however, you can use the following list. Roll 2d6 and add the Amity of the main PC engaging with the other characters.

- ✹ 2-4: Instant total hostility, characters attack
- ✹ 5-8: Hostile wariness, will cautiously watch the PCs
- ✹ 9-12: Uncertain or uncaring, reaction depends on role-play
- ✹ 13-15: Affable, will consider reasonable offers
- ✹ 16+: Characters seek friendship with PCs

DAMAGE AND INJURY

DAMAGE

When your character hits another character in combat, they do damage to that character's hit points. Your character's weapon or power will show you what to roll for damage. Add your character's GRIT to melee damage. Subtract this damage from your opponent's HP.

If this reduces their HP to 0 or lower, you have caused your opponent an *injury*. Any damage taken when a character's

HP are at 0 causes another injury. Foes at 0 HP are more likely to surrender, and at the GM's discretion characters using Amity or intimidation against them have a DC 5 easier than normal.

An example: the outlaw Tim Killian is holed up in a barn, wounded to 0 HP but armed with dynamite and a whole lot of ammo. The preacher tries to talk him into giving up. Killian's wanted for murder and is facing the gallows, so the DC would normally be Very Hard (DC 25). Since he's at 0 HP, the DC is reduced to DC 20. Good thing that preacher has a high Amity...

Unnamed characters and monsters (such as harpies or giant ants) often die at 0 HP instead of taking injuries, unless it's a dramatic fight against a few monsters and the GM feels like keeping track of monster injuries. Undead always die at 0 HP.

CRITICAL HITS

If you roll a 20 when seeing if your character hits their opponent, your character makes a critical hit. Roll your damage normally. The opponent takes this damage and also takes an injury.

INJURIES

Roll 2d6 and consult the Injury Table to see the effects of a character's injury. If the character already has an injury currently affecting them, add 1 to the result for each previous injury they're still suffering from. Certain other situations, like gun duels, may modify the results. All of these options are abstract and should be described by the GM and players as it makes sense.

Upon suffering a broken or severed limb, broken ribs, or fatal wound, a character is in shock. Each round they can test Toughness + GRIT versus a DC of 15 in order to overcome the shock and take some action.

INJURY TABLE

Roll	Effect
2	no effect
3	stunned, lose next action
4	knocked down
5	knocked down & stunned
6	minor injury, knocked out for 2d6 rounds
7	serious injury (broken limb, punctured artery, lodged bullet), 1d6+2 days to heal, *bleeding*
8	major injury (broken ribs, perforated lung, lodged bullet), 2d6+4 days to heal, *bleeding*
9	multiple major injuries or gruesome injury (severed limb, knee shot out), 2d8+6 days to heal, will never be 100% (exact effects up to GM), *bleeding*
10	deadly wound, will die in 3d6 rounds unless bleeding stopped, will likely lose limb
11	fatal wound (gutted, stabbed through the heart, broken neck or back, etc), will die in 2d6 rounds
12+	instant death

TEMPORARY HIT POINTS

If a character has *temporary hit points* (usually due to a preacher's prayer), damage comes off of these temporary hit points first. Temporary hit points never stack. For instance, if a character has 6 temporary hit points and a preacher *inspires* her for 10 temporary hit points, the character has 10 temporary hit points and not 14. Hit points lost due to using powers ignore temporary hit points and always come off of real hit points.

Example: The preacher Jebidiah has 3 HP and 8 Temp HP. He intones a 2nd rank prayer that does 5 points of damage to him. He now has -2 HP, 8 Temp HP, and he passes out for 2d6 rounds (as described under Powers) because his HP have dropped below 0. He wakes up just as he is stabbed by a dog-gobbler for 4 pts of damage. Jebidiah now has -2 HP and 4 Temp HP. He's still on his feet. Another dog-gobbler chews on his neck for 6 points of damage. Jebidiah now has -4 HP, 0 Temp HP, and suffers an injury. Let's hope he's made his peace with the All-Mighty...

HEALING AND RECOVERY

Preachers can bring a character back to consciousness and grant temporary hit points. A character can recover all their HP by having a solid meal and getting a good night's sleep. Sleeping 3 hours on the trail between eating a pot of old beans and getting attacked by a native band of shee doesn't count.

Injuries take a good while to heal, as shown on the Injury Table. They will only heal correctly if set by someone with some medic training. Otherwise, a character will be crippled for life.

A character who has dealt with injured folk before can try to reduce the time it takes to heal. Each day, they can make a Learning +WITS test versus 10 + the number of days left to heal. If they succeed, that day counts as 2 days (3 if the patient is an orc).

GUNSHOTS AND STABBINGS

Almost all puncture wounds will induce bleeding, as will stabbings. When taking an injury from a gunshot or stabbing, any result on the injury table that ends with *bleeding* results in serious bleeding that will eventually result in death if not stopped. If a bullet is lodged in the wound, it must be removed to prevent infection. To keep the injured above snakes, the wound must be heavily wrapped in the case of a serious injury, or have a tourniquet applied or be cauterized in the case of an even worse injury. A tourniquet can only be used on a limb, and that limb will almost certainly be lost.

ABILITY DAMAGE

Conditions like bleeding, disease and exposure can lower ability scores. Characters are unable to function once an ability score hits -5. For GRIT, this means death; for DRAW, it means tremors or paralysis; for WITS, it means catatonia or insanity. As an ability score approaches -5, symptoms such as coughing, shaking hands or raving are clearly visible to an observer. Ability scores cannot drop below -5.

It is up to the GM as to how quickly lost ability scores recover. For temporary loss, recovery usually happens at 1 point/day for each ability. For a more serious loss due to disease, the recovery drops to 1 point/week for each ability.

CHAPTER EIGHT
FIGHTING

Combat is conducted in *rounds*. Rounds are an abstract measure of time, usually between 2 and 10 seconds. Where necessary, assume ten rounds take about a minute.

ZONES

In combat, the landscape your characters are on is split up into *zones*. Zones are areas demarcated by natural barriers or by the general length a character could run in 5-10 seconds. For instance, in a bar fight the barroom would be one zone, the 2nd floor balcony overhead a second, and the porch outside the saloon a third.

Missile weapons have a range they can fire under ideal conditions. Your character can fire one zone further than their weapon's range with a -2 penalty, and 1 zone closer with a -5 penalty. They cannot fire more than one zone closer or past their weapon's range.

ACTIONS

Your character can perform one of the following *combat actions* each round:

* Swing a weapon, throw a punch, or the like
* Shoot a gun, crossbow, bow, or throw a weapon
* Reload a weapon
* Provide cover fire
* Light an explosive's fuse
* Use a skill
* Use a power
* Use a piece of equipment

In addition, your character may move from one zone to an adjacent one before or after their combat action. If you declare they are taking this action, your character gains the *trailin'* status.

Your character can *dive for cover* for free during a round, giving them +2 bonus to Defense for partial cover or +5 bonus to Defense for total cover (which will affect who they can attack). Other free actions include talking and standing up. Your character can also draw a weapon and run within their current zone zone, although each of these slows them down a bit, as explained below.

TRAILIN'

Trailin' characters suffer a -2 penalty to Defense. If another character is providing cover fire for them, as noted below, this penalty is negated.

A trailin' character acts last in initiative order, going only after all non-trailin' characters have finished their actions. If your character is already trailin' for some reason, they can only change zones by giving up their combat action for the round.

This sort of initiative system works best when players make their declaration nice and broad. If there are six cowboy bandits, players should say "I'm going to shoot a bandit" instead of "I'm going to shoot the third hombre on the left." Other examples might be "I'm diving for cover and lighting a stick of dynamite," only worrying about where that dynamite is going to be thrown when the player's turn comes up. That way players can quickly give a sketch of their intent, and worry about details as their turn approaches.

ORDER OF ACTIONS IN A ROUND

At the beginning of each round, all players and the GM must declare what their characters are doing. The side with more characters in total declares first.

After all actions are declared, each player rolls *initiative* for their character, which is a d6 + DRAW. The higher DRAW wins ties unless a character is using a quick-draw-style holster; if DRAW is tied as well, PCs act before NPCs or monsters. The GM can roll for each of their characters, or if there is a group of like characters, they can roll once for the whole group. Subtract 1 from your character's initiative for each of the following they are doing:

* Drawing a weapon
* Moving within a zone
* Using a rifle
* Using a heavy melee weapon

If an action before your character's prevents their declared action, and they are not already trailin', you may revise your declaration. Your character gains the trailin' status.

Conduct each character's action in order from the highest initiative to the lowest initiative, among those who are not trailin'. Next, conduct each trailin' character's action in order from the highest initiative to the lowest initiative.

A character who is providing cover fire is assumed to be doing so for the whole round.

ATTACKING

If your character attacks in melee, throws or fires a missile weapon, or uses a power against someone else, you must make an *attack roll*. Roll a d20 and add the appropriate attack bonus. If your character is attacking with a melee or missile weapon, you must roll equal to or greater than their opponent's Defense score in order to hit the opponent. If your character is using a power, that power will tell you what defense score you must roll equal to or greater than. If you hit, see *Damage and Injury* to see what to do. If you roll a 20 on the d20 before adding the attack bonus, your character scores a *critical hit* on their opponent. If this happens, your opponent takes normal damage and also suffers an injury. See the earlier section *Damage and Injuries* for details.

While Trailin' is a perfectly good term for going last in a round, the traditional Old West phrase is "sucking hind tit." We considered using this in the rules instead, but better sense prevailed.

There's an easy way to remember who's trailin' every round. Keep a bowl nearby filled with some sort of markers - poker chips, glass beads, or coins. If someone acquires the trailin' status, give them a marker. Run through initiative for everyone without a marker, then run through it for everyone with one.

Initiative is a d6 + DRAW. The fastest way to run initiative is for the GM to say a high number, usually "10 or higher?", and have those people act. Then the GM counts down. "9s." "8s." "7s." Players and NPCs go when their number is called. If someone starts trailin' or begins to dither about what they want to do, hand them a marker and come back to them at the end of the round.

COVER FIRE

Cover fire helps protect vulnerable allies, usually when they're moving and exposing themselves to their foes. In order to provide cover fire, your character must have a gun (or other ranged weapon). Your character can provide cover fire for one other character who is moving. If any other character shoots at them while they are moving, your character can fire at the shooter first. You can still only shoot once in a round. If you are providing cover fire for a character, you remove any Defense penalty they are suffering due to trailin'.

Example: Clara's normal Defense is 15, but she's trailin', so her Defense drops to 13 as she leaps off that balcony. If one of her friends is providing cover fire, blasting away with a six-gun at anyone who threatens her, they negate the trailin' Defense penalty and Clara's Defense rises back up to 15.

HIDING BEHIND COVER

Characters can dive for cover in their current zone as a free action during a combat round, and that's usually a good idea. Cover may be an object like a door, a barrel, rocks, or a horse (which usually ends poorly for the horse). A character behind partial cover gains a +2 to their defenses and can attack others with no penalty. A character behind total cover gains a +5 to their defenses, and the GM may rule that they can't be successfully attacked at all, but they can't attack anyone they're covered from.

If you find you're getting hit too often, remember to use cover.

An example: Cletus is playing poker in the saloon when a bandit walks in and open fire with pistols. As a free action in his combat round Cletus flips the table over. He gains +2 Defense against the bandit's gunfire and can fire on the bandit without penalty. The next round Cletus dives behind the bar. He gains +5 to his Defense, but the GM decides he could still be targeted because the bandit can shoot the bottles above the bar to rain glass down on the hidden gunslinger. Cletus can't target the bandit until he or the bandit moves.

PENALTIES

There may be other circumstances that make actions in combat more difficult; darkness, earthquakes, collapsing mines, fighting on horseback, and the like.

EXAMPLE OF INITIATIVE

Bryce draws his pistol, runs across the saloon, dives behind the bar for cover, and shoots at a masked bandit. He's only moved within one zone, so he acts on his initiative -2. He'd rolled a 7 on his d6 + DRAW, so he goes on 5.

Jane planned to draw her gun and shoot the same bandit, but Bryce killed him. Jane picks a new action to grab the cashbox from the unattended bar instead. On her initiative of 4, Jane takes the trailin' status. The GM gives her a trailin' token to remind her. She'll act like the scoundrel she is once everyone in the fight who isn't trailin' has gone. While she's trailin', her Defense drops by -2.

Like Jane, Quentin had intended to move and attack the bandit Bryce killed, but a low DRAW means his initiative after a -1 modifier is 3. He picks a new action, which makes him trailin',

and he decides to run through the saloon doors into the street outside. That's another zone. Since Quentin is already trailin' he'll have to give up his combat action to change zones. At the end of the round after Jane acts, he sprints across the bar and bursts outside. His Defense is at -2 until his turn next round.

Clara wants to dive off the saloon's balcony and tackle another bandit off his horse. Her initiative is 2. She is moving from one zone to another so she gains the trailin' status. Once everyone in the fight who isn't trailin' has gone, and once Jane and Quentin have gone (since their initiatives were higher than Clara's), she'll make her leap and try to tackle the bandit. Let's hope he stays put; because she's already trailin', Clara can't choose another action if the bandit happens to ride off on his turn.

At the GM's discretion, moderate difficulties impose a -2 penalty to attacks or grant a +2 bonus to defenses, and severe difficulties raise this modifier to -5 or +5.

FIRING INTO A CROWD

If your character fires into a crowd, their target is considered to have partial cover, giving them +2 to Defense. If your character misses, they have a 50% chance to hit a random bystander.

SURPRISE

Surprise is rolled when an opponent might not know his foe is there. This usually occurs when one person is sneaking up on another or is waiting in ambush, but mutual surprise is possible. A character needs to pass a Wile + DRAW check versus an opponent's Mental Defense in order to surprise them. A surprised character is trailin' for the first round of combat.

That means the surprised side automatically goes after the unsurprised side (unless someone on the unsurprised side is moving a zone, in which case they might fall somewhere in the middle of the surprised team's initiative order). Characters on the surprised side are limited to what they can do, since they can only take a combat action OR move a zone while trailin'.

When the situation is more complicated, like two groups on horseback suddenly meeting at a pass, one person on each side rolls a Wile + DRAW skill check versus the other person's mental defense. Success means that other side is surprised and is automatically trailin' for the first round. If both sides are surprised, just skip to combat-as-usual.

EXAMPLE OF SURPRISE

The PCs are headed up Hangman's Gulch and are not being very stealthy. Outlaw sentries are skulking behind rocks; the GM rolls Wile + DRAW against the PCs' best Mental Defense, and beats it. The PCs are surprised.

"You're making your way up the canyon. In places you need to clamber over rockfalls or ease your way past boulders. Suddenly there's a whoop from somewhere ahead and above you and shots ring out! You're surprised. Roll initiative… and for the first round, you're all trailin'. What are your actions?"

There's nothing for the PCs to shoot at yet, so they declare that they're taking partial cover, drawing pistols, and shooting at anyone who comes within range. If a smart PC correctly suspects that the outlaws are using rifles with a much longer range than a pistol, and are unlikely to approach, she'll dive behind a larger boulder that gives total cover instead. That +5 to Defense will buy some time while the PCs figure out whether to retreat.

CHAPTER NINE
GUNFIGHTER DUELS

A classic staple of Western movies is the gunfight. Two gunfighters stand on a dusty street. Tumbleweed blows between them. They stare each other in the eye, slowly easing open their coats to get to their holsters, fingers flexing... When it's over, one man is dead on the ground, and the gravedigger has a new job.

The basic rules for *Owl Hoot Trail* combat don't allow for this sort of duel, unless you're a gunfighter lucky enough to score an injury on their first shot. These optional rules give your PCs a chance to die gloriously in duels with strangers. If you're going to die, you might as well go out memorably.

DUELS

Unless the GM decides otherwise, duels can happen only by mutual consent. Use normal combat rules for ambushes or any gunfights that aren't arranged. Most monsters can not and will not duel; depending on their personality, intelligent humanoid monsters such as vampires might be an exception.

Anyone can duel so long as they have a missile weapon and the willingness to face their own mortality. Duels normally occur with the gunfighters separated by 1 zone. Traditionally this is an open area - a dusty street, a graveyard, a dried out riverbed - where there are no obstructions or accidental targets.

A duel is divided into two portions: staredown and gunplay.

STAREDOWN

The two (or more if the GM allows) gunmen stare each other down, likely contemplating death. Each duelist rolls an opposed check of a d20 + Wile + GRIT. The winner gains +2 on initiative.

GUNPLAY

The gunmen roll initiative normally, d6 + DRAW. The winner of the Buildup adds +2. If a tie, the higher DRAW goes first; if DRAW is tied, gunplay is simultaneous unless one character is using a quick-draw-style holster. As usual, drawing a weapon or using a rifle subtracts 1 from each character's initiative.

All shots fired by a duelist during this first round of combat are automatically considered critical hits, with +3 added to the injury roll. If hit in the first round, a combatant loses his next action in addition to any other effect of the injury.

Duels only last for one round, and it's generally considered that the first person to hit the other has won. If hostilities continue after the first round, combat reverts to normal non-dueling rules.

CHAPTER TEN
FOES AND MONSTERS

Humanoid foes can be created using the normal character creation system. For creatures, assign them abilities and a level. If it makes sense, give them powers or increased scores. Normal creatures get 5 HP per level; giant creatures and undead get 7 HP per level. The formula for HP is 10 + GRIT + (level - 1) x5 or 7.) Intelligent creatures get +3 to one skill. Creatures can also be cowpokes, with only 1 HP regardless of level, or cowpunchers, requiring two hits of any kind or one injury to kill.

You can increase the level of any creature by adding levels. For every doubling of the creature's level, increase the die size of their damage (d4 goes to d6, d6 goes to d8, and so on.)

Monsters have three named traits that affect their injury rolls, *Sickly*, *Hardy* and *Deadly*.

* Creatures labelled *Sickly* add the listed value to any injury roll they are forced to make. For instance, Giant Ants are Sickly 2. Score an injury on them while fighting, and a roll of 4 (knocked down) would become a roll of 6 (minor injury, knocked out.)
* Creatures labelled *Hardy* subtract the listed points from any injuries they receive. Hardy monsters are often boss monsters. For instance, an ogre has Hardy 1; score a serious injury on them with a roll of 7, and

it becomes a minor injury instead when the roll is downgraded to 6.

* Creatures labelled *Deadly* add the listed value to any injury roll they inflict. For instance, prairie trolls are notoriously deadly. Their Deadly 1 turns a gruesome injury of 9 into a deadly wound of 10.

Some monsters have conditions on these traits. For instance, a hangman tree is Hardy 2, except to fire or explosives, against which it is Sickly 2. If you run up against a hangman tree, you're always best off keeping your distance and burning it out. Werewolves work the same way against silver.

The undead do not receive injuries. They collapse at 0 HP.

Ant, Giant: where there's one giant ant, there's probably a whole anthill.

Lvl 3, GRIT 0, DRAW 2, WITS -2, HP 20, Def 15, MDef 11. Bite +3 (1d6). *Sickly 2.*

Bat, Giant: swooping through the night and picking off its prey.

Lvl 2, GRIT 0, DRAW 1, WITS -3, HP 15, Def 16, MDef 9. Bite +2 (1d4). *Sickly 1.*

Bear, Black: more afraid of you than you are of him.

Lvl 4, GRIT 4, DRAW 2, WITS -2, HP 29, Def 16, MDef 12. Claw +8 (1d6+4) with followup bite +8 (1d8).

Bear, Cave: ancient throwback of teeth, muscle and claw.

Lvl 7, GRIT 5, DRAW 2, WITS 0, HP 45, Def 19, MDef 17. Claw +12 (1d10+4) with followup claw +12 with followup bite +9 (1d12); or roar attack +12, causes all affected foes in its or adjacent zones to be automatically trailin' for the next two rounds.

Chupacabra: they're mysterious only because they kill everyone who sees them. Given their choice, they prefer to eat people who haven't bathed.

Lvl 8, GRIT 4, DRAW 5, WITS 1, HP 54, Def 23, MDef 19. Claw +12 (1d8+4) with followup bite +13 (2d6) or throw +12 (thrown 1d12 + 4 yards, take that much damage). *Hardy 1, Deadly 1.*

Creek demon: a lost spirit of Hell, rising from water and disappearing at dawn.

Lvl 3, GRIT 3, DRAW 1, WITS 3, HP 23, Def 14, MDef 16. Claw +6 (1d6+4); spitting cold green hellfire +4 (range 0-1, 1d6).

Dog-gobbler: they eat dogs first, but that's so nothing barks when they come for the children.

Lvl 1, GRIT -1, DRAW 1, WITS 2, HP 9, Def 12, MDef 13. Bite +0 (1d6-1); trick +3 (*Silent Illusion*, *Sleep*, *Ventriloquism*). Can *teleport*, but only to nearby small, dark places such as closets or under beds. *Sickly 1.*

Goblin: tunnelling through foothills and destroying all they see.

Lvl 1, GRIT 0, DRAW 2, WITS 1, HP 10, Def 13, MDef 12. Weapon +1. In groups of three, each gains +1 to weapon and defense.

CUSTOMIZING MONSTERS

These monster descriptions are bare-boned, and you are encouraged to customize monsters to fit your *Owl Hoot Trail* campaign. For instance, consider the harpy.

You know the classic role of buzzards in the Western setting... lurking patiently in the background, waiting for someone to die? What if harpies filled a similar role? Rather than feral predators who attack with talons, they are carrion scavengers who feast on the carcasses of those already dead.

Unlike buzzards, harpies are smart enough to talk on a basic, savage level, so while a character is crawling through the desert dying of thirst, there are a couple of harpies perched on a cactus nearby giving a running commentary. Exhorting them to just give up already. Making wagers on whether they'll make it another hour, or only fifteen minutes.

Also unlike buzzards, they have some tricks to encourage the odd dead carcass. Harpies will hang out on the prairie with a little spade, looking for horses or cows - herds of wild mustangs, a cattle drive, a hard-riding posse, a stagecoach - and will fly out ahead on their likely route to dig a bunch of gopher-holes somewhere in front of them. If a horse steps in a hole and breaks its leg, it's only a matter of time. If the man riding the horse was relying on it to reach his destination before he runs out of water, two for the price of one!

But the main reason there's a bounty on harpies anywhere near civilized settlements, and the reason the natives shoot to kill on sight, is that harpies have access to a shaman curse. They can magically foul all the water in a given area. One of their favorite ploys is to stake out a watering hole in the desert. When they foul the only source of water for miles, it's easy to leave the animals who rely on it gasping and expiring within a day or two. When the water they foul supplies a settlement or town, it can potentially spell doom for the whole population, so they're ruthlessly culled whenever they make an appearance. For the lone traveler making his way from town to town, it doesn't matter how much water he's carrying with him if it gets hexed and becomes undrinkable. After that, the harpies just need to follow him (jeering and insulting him the whole way) until the inevitable occurs.

Follow this example with other monsters whenever you think an encounter could be more exciting. The better a monster fits into your campaign, the more memorable it will become.

Ghoul: cannibals and gluttons rise up from the grave.

Lvl 3, GRIT 2, DRAW 1, WITS -1, HP 26, Def 14, MDef 12. Claw +4 (1d4+2, Toughness + GRIT vs DC 12 + ghoul's level test, paralyzed for 1d6 rounds on failure); or weapon. Eats human flesh. *Undead.*

Hangman Tree: the fruit looks delicious, but careful where you walk.

Lvl 5, GRIT 5, DRAW -3, WITS -1, HP 43, Def 12, MDef 14. Strangle x4 +10 (1d6 each and lift from ground.) *Hardy 2; against fire or explosives, Sickly 2.*

Harpy: feral scavengers who foul water holes and prey on the dead.

Lvl 2, GRIT 2, DRAW 2, WITS -1, HP 17, Def 14, MDef 11. Claws +4 (1d6+2); or screech attack +1 (mentalist trick *hypnotism*). Given a few minutes to work their curse, harpies can magically foul water supplies in a zone.

Hellhound: the Adversary's hounds, set loose upon the world.

Lvl 5, GRIT 3, DRAW 1, WITS 2, HP 33, Def 16, MDef 17. Bite +8 (1d6+3) with followup slam +8 (1d6+3 and knocked prone.)

Landshark: burrowing beneath the grasslands in search of easy prey.

Lvl 5, GRIT 5, DRAW -1, WITS -1, HP 35, Def 19 or 14 (belly), MDef 14. Bite +10 (1d8+5) with followup claw (1d6+5). Armored plates give near complete cover (Def +5) to every part except its belly and the inside of its mouth. *Hardy 1.*

Leech, Giant: stay out of still water.

Lvl 1, GRIT 1, DRAW -4, WITS -4, HP 11, Def 8, MDef 8. Sneak attack +2 vs. MDef (1d4+1), keep leeching blood automatically every round after that (1d4). If ripped off, 1d6 damage to victim. Can be burnt off. *Sickly 3.*

Mummy: sometimes, the native tribes left terrible guardians behind.

Lvl 6, GRIT 4, DRAW 0, WITS 1, HP 49, Def 16, MDef 17. Slam +10 (1d8+4) with followup punch or choke +10 (1d6+4, 1d4 rot damage for the next 1d4 rounds). If killed by a mummy, you become its undead slave. *Undead.*

Ogre: twice the size of a man, and more than twice as cruel.

Lvl 6, GRIT 6, DRAW 2, WITS -1, HP 51, Def 18, MDef 15. Slam +12 (1d10+6) or by weapon; thrown half-eaten sheep carcass +8 (1d8). *Hardy 1. Giant.*

Owlbear: if it doesn't kill you itself, the creatures drawn by its plaintive cry will.

Lvl 9, GRIT 5, DRAW 2, WITS 3, HP 55, Def 21, MDef 22. Claw +14 (1d8+5) with follow-up claw +14; with followup hug +11 (2d8+5); or Howl of Lament +12, all intelligent creatures within earshot who are affected are saddened and automatically trailin' for the next two rounds. All wild creatures who hear it come to see.

Rat, Goliath: the piranhas of the prairie. Afraid of fire and full of disease, a swarm of goliath rats can chew through a horse in minutes.

Lvl 2, GRIT 0, DRAW 2, WITS -3, HP 1 (cowpoke), Def 14, MDef 9. Bite +2 (1d4, plus possible disease). Ratbite fever lowers GRIT and WITS by -1 each week until cured by a sawbones or preacher. If bit, roll a DC 15 Toughness + GRIT check at end of combat to stay healthy.

Rattlesnake: listen for the rattle.

Lvl 1, GRIT 0, DRAW 2, WITS -3, HP 11, Def 13, MDef 8. Bite +1 (1d3, plus 1d6 poison damage each hour for the next 1d4 hours.)

Sand Dragon: you can lose a whole herd to one of these.

Lvl 10, GRIT 8, DRAW 3, WITS 4, HP 81, Def 23, MDef 24. Crush +18 (1d12+8); or tail grab +13 (1d12) with followup fling +13 (2d6+8 or 1d6+4 if missed); or sand blast +18 (3d6 to all in front of it; can use once every 1d6 rounds.) *Hardy 2, Deadly 2.*

Skeeters: mosquitoes grow pretty damn big out here.

Lvl 3, GRIT 0, DRAW 5, WITS -3, HP 1 (cowpoke), Def 18, MDef 10. Proboscis +5 (1d4 and clings to prey), keep leeching blood automatically every round after that (1d4).

Skeleton: worms have taken the flesh, but bone and hatred remain.

Lvl 1, GRIT 1, DRAW 1, WITS -3, HP 11, Def 14, MDef 8. Weapon +2 (dam +1). *Undead.*

COWPOKES

Western movies are famous for unnamed extras who, shot once, die in a spectacular and cinematic manner. *Owl Hoot Trail* is no different. We call these cowpokes, and they always have only 1 hit point. All of their other combat statistics are normal for their race, class, and level. This allows them to remain a threat but still be killed with a single shot. A NPC of any level can be a cowpoke. In general, as soon as a NPC is given a name they stop being a cowpoke (although they may become a cowpuncher if the GM so decides.)

COWPUNCHERS

Like cowpokes, cowpunchers are nameless extras who are destined to die spectacularly when shot at by your players. They're a little tougher than cowpokes, however; cowpunchers must be hit twice before they die. The first hit visibly wounds them, no matter how much damage it inflicts, and the second hit kills them - usually so that they can crash through a window, fall off a roof, or be dragged to death by a horse.

Cowpunchers die immediately if they ever receive an injury or a critical hit. They know their job, and they stick to it.

Spectre: a hungry soul that hates the living.

Lvl 4, GRIT 3, DRAW 2, WITS 1, HP 34, Def 16, MDef 15. Soul-suck +7 vs MDef (1d8). Cannot be harmed by normal weapons. *Undead.*

Spider, Giant: whether hunting spider, trapdoor spider, or web builder, you don't want to get mistaken as prey.

Lvl 6, GRIT 1, DRAW 5, WITS -1, HP 36, Def 21, MDef 15. Shoot web +11 (1d6, range 0-1) with followup entangle +7 (lose next action); or bite +7 (1d6+1, plus 1d6 poison damage for the next 1d4 rounds.)

Troll, Prairie: stupid and bestial, with a very big club.

Lvl 4, GRIT 4, DRAW 0, WITS -1, HP 35, Def 14, MDef 13. Treetrunk club +8 (1d12+4, plus flung into the next zone if the prairie troll desires.) *Deadly 1. Giant.*

Vampire: nights are long on the prairie, and there are few trees to use for carving stakes.

Lvl 4, GRIT 2, DRAW 3, WITS 3, HP 33, Def 17, MDef 17. Slam +6 (1d6+2); or weapon; or grapple +6 (1d4) with followup bite +6 (1d6 and adds to vampire's HP.) Some vampires also have mentalist powers. *Undead.*

Werewolf: time to make silver bullets.

Lvl 3, GRIT 4, DRAW 3, WITS 2, HP 24, Def 16, MDef 15. Claw +7 (1d8+4). Heals 4 HP a round unless wounded with silver. *Against injury with a silver weapon, Sickly 3.*

Wolf: a plague on sheep and cattle. Unlike real-world wolves, these attack people.

Lvl 2, GRIT 2, DRAW 2, WITS -1, HP 17, Def 14, MDef 11. Bite +4 (1d6+2).

Zombie: the grave can't hold some people down.

Lvl 2, GRIT 4, DRAW -1, WITS -4, HP 21, Def 9 (includes penalty for always trailin'), MDef 8. Slam +6 (1d6 +4) or weapon. Zombies are always trailin'. Note: for an easier to kill zombie horde that's still scary, keep some zombies as regular monsters and turn some into cowpunchers who get hit, drop, then get up again. *Undead.*

CHAPTER ELEVEN

RUNNING THE GAME

In the *How to Play* section, the GM's job is summarized as the following:

* Decide on Realism.
* Build the world.
* Make up situations.
* Set up the adventure.
* Give the players hell.
* Reward the players.

How to do each of these has been touched on in the rest of this game, but we'll expand on them here.

DECIDE ON REALISM

Owl Hoot Trail is meant to be simple and cinematic, not realistic, but that doesn't mean there aren't different amounts of magic you can use. You can run this game with different levels of fantasy, from almost a straight and traditional western to a gonzo, over-the-top level of magic.

DAMN NEAR REALISTIC

Take any classic Western movie and add rare, minor magic. Forbid character classes that are overtly magical, and make the existence of magic in the campaign world a big deal. Preachers might cleave to real-world religions or their fictional analogues, and most folk the PCs meet won't believe that magic even exists. For additional realism, do some research on actual times and places in the Old West and use that information as inspiration for the game (not a bad idea regardless.)

HORROR AND WONDER

The accompanying adventure *They Rode for Perdition* assumes this degree of magic. Fantastical creatures exist and affect the world, and the world prepares for them (such as towns killing harpies on sight to protect their fresh water supplies.) Heaven and Hell are real places, and demons exist in the dark places of the world. Monsters stalk the prairies, no one trusts a known mentalist, and gadgeteers may create clockwork devices that confound your average cattleman.

MAGIC, LIKE DUST

In this high-magic world every grain of dust might carry magic in it. Everyone knows that preachers speak with the word of the Gods, ranchers have herds of pegasi or unicorns, tribes of centaurs confound expansion into the wild places, and railroads run on steam elementals. In a high-magic world, evil gadgeteers plot to conquer towns by constructing massive clockwork monstrosities, anti-charm poker decks protect against cheating mentalists, and anyone with enough cash can order a magical revolver from a local artificer. The traditional problem with a high-magic setting is that if you aren't careful, you quickly lose the starkness and solitude that typify the traditional Western setting; things just get silly. That's worth keeping in mind as you plan your game.

BUILD THE WORLD

Take something in the world and twist it. For instance:

* What would happen if a necromancer settled into a small western town and turned all its citizens into vampires? Perhaps they run out of prey and start turning on themselves and on harpies, until the PCs come into town...

* Cowboys versus the native tribes is the classic Western theme. What happens when the native tribes of many races band together under a strong war-chieftain to wipe out the newcomers, and the PCs are forced to become diplomats?

* Shamans speak to the world around them through their spirits. What would happen if the PCs were hired to prove that a famous shaman was

actually a charlatan?

* Everyone loves bank robberies and stage coach robberies - well, everyone who isn't getting robbed, that is. What happens to the PCs' plans when the local bank hires "security specialists" from out of town to protect their money, and the PCs find out that these specialists are planning a robbery themselves?

MAKE UP SITUATIONS

A situation isn't anything more than when one fellow wants something and another fellow doesn't want to let that happen. The key for running the game is to put the players' characters in the thick of it. Think about some of your favorite novels or movies for ideas. Some generic ones are:

* Some bad guys plan to rob a bank/ saloon/town/castle that the PCs are guarding.

* A group of pilgrims needs safe passage through some rough territory.

* A prospector wants a mine cleared out of critters and worse things.

* The PCs are stranded and need shelter; whoever lives in the closest shelter isn't friendly.

* And there's always Old Faithful: there's some treasure to be had and the PCs aim to have it.

This last one has an interesting twist in a Western story: *there's a reward out for delivering a wanted man to the law dead or alive*. GMs should feel free to use the hell out of this. It's the Western equivalent of a cloaked man in a fantasy bar with a job that needs doing. The PCs can't resist

it. Recommended rewards are $100 for your run of the mill bandit, up to $5,000 or even $10,000 for a body so infamous that the sun darkens at their name.

SET UP THE ADVENTURE

There's not a lot to this in *Owl Hoot Trail*. Characters and creatures are easy to build. Before play, make all the characters you think you'll need. You can keep them on index cards to help during play. In addition, make up some generic statistics for level-appropriate characters. Having a generic gunslinger, shopkeep, or fast desert predator around to pull out for unexpected encounters is always helpful.

Likewise, make a list of male and female names to quickly reference during play. This way, your game doesn't pause for you to make up a name for each random character that pops up. You may also want to search the internet for "western slang" to get a feel for the language of the old west.

Maps will help your game run well. Before play, sketch out maps of major locations that you expect the characters might end up at.

GIVE THE PLAYERS HELL

During the game, you're going to have to play all the characters that the PCs interact with. Make the ones that are friendly to the PCs plenty helpful. Few things are as frustrating as a game where you've got to pry every last nugget of information out of each character. Friendly characters should talk freely.

Unfriendly characters, however, should be dangerous and crafty.

Humans and their ilk will lie, cheat, lay traps, and worse. Monsters are just as bad. A vampire with WITS 3 is smarter than most PCs. Use that to your advantage.

Something to watch out for is railroading. This is when you've got a plan of how an adventure's going to go ahead of time, and you use your power to force the PCs into that plan. They will resist, as they should. The players are going to be wily and try to find ways out of the danger you have planned for them. Be ready for that. By having crafty foes that think and react, you can avoid railroading.

REWARD THE PLAYERS

There're three major rewards for players and their characters: experience points, treasure, and status. Experience points have a system outlined in the Advancement section. Feel free to give small spot XP bonuses for smart ideas or good roleplaying. Judge the difficulty of challenges after they are completed. Something that seemed deadly at first might be simple, or vice versa. Challenges are usually the same difficulty for all characters involved, but that doesn't have to be true.

Keep a close eye on treasure. You want to reward the players, but part of the fun of the game is managing resources. Keep treasure reasonable. A good rule of thumb is about $100-200 per PC level per adventure.

Lastly, make the PCs famous or infamous. They are Big Men or Women and bartenders, hoteliers, and shopkeeps will notice that. As they adventure more, let their legend grow and even give them leverage when talking with folks.

CHAPTER TWELVE
RESOURCES

NAMES

To come up with names for characters quickly, you can use this chart. Roll d100 three times: once for a nickname, once for a first name, and once for a last name.

	Nickname	First name (male)	First name (female)	Last name
1	Apples	Abelino	Alicia	Acord
2	Astral	Abraham	Amanda	Allen
3	Avenging	Addison	Amelia	Austin
4	Backwards	Alejandro	Ana	Autry
5	Bandit	Allan	Autumn	Baehr
6	Bat	Allison	Avery	Baggins
7	Big	Andy	Belle	Baker
8	Black	Artemus	Betty	Ballew
9	Blue	Audie	Beverly	Bannon
10	Bohemian	Beau	Billie	Barrow
11	Bottomless	Berry	Bly	Barry
12	Broncho	Bill	Bobbie	Barton
13	Buzz	Billy	Bonnie	Bennett
14	Calamity	Bob	Bryce	Blake
15	Cherry	Bose	Carmela	Blankenship
16	Chili	Bryce	Carolina	Boone
17	Crash	Buck	Cat	Bow
18	Cupcake	Buddy	Charity	Browne

19	Deadeye	Calvin	Cheyenne	Carpenter
20	Deadwood	Cecil	Clementine	Cash
21	Doc	Chuck	Cody	Chandler
22	Dogface	Clay	Connie	Coldren
23	Doomsday	Clayton	Crystal	Connors
24	Dragon	Clint	Daisy	Corrigan
25	Ears	Cooper	Dakota	Derringer
26	Elephant	Cord	Dale	Devine
27	Evil	Cyril	Doli	Díaz
28	Faerie	David	Domino	Dooley
29	Fingers	Dennis	Dorothy	Dreisbach
30	Flagpole	Domingo	Dusty	Earp
31	Flapjack	Don	Echo	Elfborn
32	Fuzzy	Douglas	Elvira	Elliott
33	Giddy	Duncan	Engracia	Farseer
34	Goblin	Dusty	Esmeralda	Fearslayer
35	Golden	Elfego	Evelyn	Ford
36	Green	Ernesto	Frances	Frazee
37	Handsome	Fernando	Frankie	Garner
38	Haunted	Flint	Gabby	Gómez
39	Heck	Francis	Gail	Gore
40	Hoot	Gabby	Glory	Gravely
41	Hoss	Gabriel	Grace	Grey
42	Iron Rations	Gary	Harley	Hammerclan
43	Ivory	Gene	Haven	Hickok
44	Jackass	George	Helen	Holt
45	Jumping	Gonzalo	Hope	Houston
46	Kid	Grady	Ione	Hunter
47	King	Gregorio	Isabella	Irondust
48	Knuckles	Grover	Jacinta	Jackson
49	Lean	Hal	Jane	Ketchum
50	Lefty	Harry	Jayna	Kimmel

51	Little	Henry	Jenny	Knight
52	Lonesome	Hollis	Jo	LaRue
53	Mack	Iñigo	Josie	Lazenby
54	Midnight	Irvine	Justice	Loving
55	Moose	Isom	Kai	Maynard
56	Naughty	Jack	Kate	McCoy
57	Nightmare	James	Kitty	McGee
58	Nine-Toes	Jason	Leah	McNutt
59	Old	Jedediah	Lemon	Mix
60	One Horse	Jesús	Liberty	Montoya
61	Paladin	Joel	Louise	Moonsinger
62	Piece of Eight	Johnny	Lucy	Moore
63	Pretty	Jorge	Lulu	Morningstar
64	Purple Worm	Josiah	Margarita	Nixon
65	Quick	Julio	Maria	O'Halloran
66	Quiet	Justice	Mary	Page
67	Rascal	Kermit	Max	Painbringer
68	Red	Kirby	Montana	Pasquale
69	Rocky	Lane	Natalia	Perrin
70	Rowdy	Lash	Nell	Pickett
71	Sassy	Leland	Oakley	Piomboeuf
72	Sharpshooter	Leo	Olathe	Porter
73	Shy	Levi	Ophelia	Randall
74	Silver	Lyle	Peggy	Ratcook
75	Slim	Manuel	Polly	Renaldo
76	Smiley	Merle	Ramona	Ritter
77	Smokey	Monte	Reese	Rogers
78	Snake	Nat	Reno	Russell
79	Sour	Otis	Rosa	Segundo
80	Sphinx	Pablo	Ruby	Shieldbearer
81	Spider	Rafael	Ruth	Skaggs
82	Standup	Randolph	Sadie	Slade

83	Steel	Ray	Sage	Slaughter
84	Sweet	Reginald	Sam	Starr
85	Tank	Remi	Sarah	Steele
86	Terrible	Rex	Shane	Stewart
87	Tumbleweed	Rod	Skye	Swordsmith
88	Ugly	Rowdy	Star	Thomson
89	Unicorn	Sergio	Sunrise	Treuer
90	Vampire	Shoat	Sunset	Tyler
91	Vicious	Simon	Susie	Waller
92	Vorpal	Smith	Tallulah	Warren
93	Whistler	Tom	Tamaya	Wayne
94	White	Tucker	Temperance	Weed
95	Wild	Valentine	Una	Whately
96	Wolf	Wally	Violeta	Wills
97	XP	Wayne	Virginia	Windrider
98	Yellow	Will	Whisper	Winters
99	Young	Wyatt	Winona	Yates
100	Zippy	Zane	Zinnia	Younce

Note that some tribes of shee use a different style of name consisting of a number, adjective, and noun. You may find shee named Three Bloody Hatchets or Ten Flying Hawks; citified shee occasionally take names such as Three Empty Bottles or Five Polished Saddles.

The following chart of shee names is far from exclusive and should be used for inspiration. Roll d20 three times; once for each portion of the name.

	First name	Second name	Third name
1	One	Ancient	Arrows
2	One	Angry	Bears
3	One	Bloody	Blades
4	Two	Brave	Bullets
5	Two	(Choose a color)	Clouds
6	Two	Clever	Days
7	Three	Crazy	Feathers
8	Three	Dancing	Flames
9	Three	Fierce	Footsteps
10	Four	Fiery	Horses

RESOURCES

11	Four	Hidden	Leaves
12	Four	Proud	Nights
13	Five	Running	Otters
14	Five	Sharp	Plagues
15	Six	Silent	Ravens
16	Six	Smiling	Rivers
17	Seven	Singing	Serpents
18	Eight	Swift	Shadows
19	Nine	Unexpected	Stars
20	Ten	Wise	Wolves

QUICK SKILL REFERENCE

These skill examples are not exclusive; you'll find lots of examples that aren't listed on this sheet. When you do, choose the combination that makes the most sense. If more than one combination of skills and abilities applies, choose the one that is most beneficial to the player.

Skill	Examples of Use
Amity + GRIT	Gathering a posse, slowly earning a NPC's respect
Amity + DRAW	Quick-witted banter, making a good first impression
Amity + WITS	Noticing lies, being persuasive
Learning + GRIT	Medical knowledge and practice
Learning + DRAW	Quoting the law, recognizing clues
Learning + WITS	Translation, history, remembering obscure lore
Toughness + GRIT	Climbing, holding up under starvation or torture, blocking a foe from leaving a zone (opposed check)
Toughness + DRAW	Dodging, wrasslin' a steer, bull-rushing a foe into a different zone (opposed check)
Toughness + WITS	Disbelieving mirages, overcoming a persistent effect
Wilderness + GRIT	Crossing a barren desert
Wilderness + DRAW	Hunting a wild animal
Wilderness + WITS	Tracking people, noticing something odd in the wilderness
Wile + GRIT	Intimidation
Wile + DRAW	Most gambling, sneaking (base DC = foe's Mental Defense)
Wile + WITS	Bluffing, cheating when gambling, perception

PART TWO
THEY RODE TO PERDITION

CHAPTER THIRTEEN
THEY RODE TO PERDITION

Up in the foothills east of Perdition there's a watering hole that's made from death. Animals come in to drink and collapse on the spot, their bodies rotting into a tangled bone fence around the pool. No one knows why; the water comes in clean, the water goes out clean, and there's no poison that anyone has ever found. Nevertheless, people stay clear. Carcass Creek is a cursed place. Bad things happen there. Bad things like this.

ADVENTURE STRUCTURE

This isn't a "follow the map" adventure. That's not how Westerns work. Instead, there's a problem in the empty little town of Perdition that different groups of people are making worse. It's up to your players to untangle the mess. This adventure is designed so that when it goes off the rails, you'll know what to do; it can't easily be broken. If they shoot down the big bad guy the first time they meet him, that's kind of fantastic. It'll change things (and not necessarily for the better as far as your players are concerned), but we'll give you the tools to figure out what happens next.

It's fine if your players don't help every potential ally or pursue every lead, faction, or villain. Give them free rein as long as they have somewhere to go and aren't standing around debating their options. Villains who aren't brought down or humbled may survive to plague the PCs in the future, and unresolved problems have a nasty way of returning worse than ever. Keep track of who survives, and you'll have adventure seeds for plenty of future games.

This adventure is broken into a structure that should make it easy to run.

* What's Going On in Perdition? A quick summary of the adventure's plot.

* Who's Who in Perdition, and what they want. All your major characters are here, as well as their goals. Understand what a person is angling for and it'll be easy for you to decide how they act when someone holds a gun to their head.

* The Adventure, split into three acts, a prologue and an epilogue. This section lists major locations the PCs are likely to go to, what's happening there now, and what the PCs are likely to find.

Throughout the adventure are adventure tips, suggestions on running *Owl Hoot Trail*, and advice on how to handle it when your PCs do something unexpected. It's expected that you will make up anything that isn't written

Perdition can be a deadly place. It's recommended that you use the *Hardened Characters* option for tougher starting PCs, giving each of the heroes starting HP of 15 + GRIT instead of 10 + GRIT. These extra 5 hit points stay with the characters as they advance in levels.

down here, and likely change half of what we've already written down for you. This is your adventure; own it and make it unique.

RUNNING TIME

Fully played out, this adventure can last four sessions or more. If you want to speed things up, the easiest method is remove most of Act Two. If the PCs immediately question the gravedigger after talking to Caledonia, and he puts them on the trail of the despicable Hank Hitchins right away, you can run a fun and satisfying adventure in four to six hours.

WHAT'S GOING ON IN PERDITION?

Most townsfolk think the biggest problem is the Killers of Carcass Creek, a gang of outlaws plaguing the town. It's difficult for folks to safely get in or out of Perdition unless they're on the local stagecoach or accompanied by a large, well-armed group. The outlaws have been robbing and murdering travelers, and the local sheriff is too damn drunk to do anything about it.

All these fresh bodies need burying, so the gravedigger has been working overtime. During the adventure, the PCs discover that these bodies are missing. The gravedigger has been filling coffins with rocks and smuggling the freshly-dead corpses out of town. To where? No one knows, and by the time this gets discovered the gravedigger has been murdered by someone who doesn't want the information getting out.

Turns out the owner of the local stagecoach has been taking and selling the corpses to a nearby tribe of native shee. The corrupted shee shaman has been creating zombies by summoning evil spirits up at Carcass Creek and sticking the spirits into already dead bodies. Her tribe sells the zombies to anyone who will buy them. A few have been sold off to a local clan of hill folk miners who use them secretly to mine gold around the clock, but more than three dozen have gone to a nearby cattle baron who has bad, bad plans for the town of Perdition. The cattle baron is working on building himself an unstoppable army that obeys his every whim.

What the cattle baron doesn't know is how his actions affect the shaman. When each of these undead is destroyed, the evil spirit that's released carries another little piece of the shaman's soul down to Hell. If the PCs and their allies manage to wipe out most of the zombies, the shaman's humanity will be forever destroyed and the demon inside of her will try to call forth the forces of Hell from Carcass Creek.

The PCs will need to uncover who's stealing corpses, why they're stealing them, and stop both the shaman and the cattle baron before their plans come to a head.

CHANGE THIS ADVENTURE

You paid for this, so it's time to make it yours. Don't follow this adventure slavishly. Hack it, change it, flip it around. Fiddle with NPC personalities. Add or cut parts of the plot. If the players like a particular NPC, lavish attention on him to make him more important to the story. Take your players' expectations and twist them; if they think Caledonia is the kindest person in town but they don't much care about Criojo, they may be out for vengeance should Caledonia get murdered and zombified. If they love Criojo and want to be outlaws instead of heroes, maybe he hires them to terrorize Perdition and then betrays them.

You're playing *Owl Hoot Trail* to have fun. If anything in this adventure gets in the way of that, shove it to the side and make up something better.

The adventure is organized in the rough order in which events might unfold, but don't expect this is exactly how your adventure will play out. Your group may decide they hate Caledonia the shopkeeper and want to ally with the evil cattle baron Criojo, or they may decide to ride out to Criojo's ranch and confront him at the beginning of Act One. That's nothing but fun, and you'll see advice throughout the adventure on how to handle situations like these.

Whatever the PCs do, there are bound to be consequences for the town. Nothing is ever easy; as the PCs uncover the mystery and deal with each group, any remaining groups react and respond intelligently.

INVOLVING YOUR PLAYERS

If you don't give the player characters an immediate hook, they're likely to start the adventure by chasing down outlaws. That's not a problem unless you're limited on time. The easiest way to quickly involve the PCs is to link them to local townsfolk. Half'lin PCs may have gotten a letter from Caledonia, for instance, and humans may have received a request from the preacher Amanda Cole that asks for their help in straightening out the sheriff. Heck, it's possible some or all of the PCs grew up there and are headed home. If your PCs are only motivated by money, they'll soon turn their sights on Alberto Criojo as the richest man in town.

You know your players better than anyone else; decide what motivates them and then tie that into the adventure's start.

USE SKILLS AND ABILITIES TO CREATE CHALLENGE

There are five skills: Amity, Learning, Toughness, Wile and Wilderness. Look for opportunities to use these skills in skill checks when interacting with NPCs and clues and something is at stake. When you do, pick the accompanying ability (GRIT, DRAW or WITS) that makes the most sense. Allow flexibility when deciding which ability to use with a skill; if a player can make a good argument for a different ability than the one you suggested, consider allowing it. The game is most fun when you reward creative play.

Don't bother requiring skill checks for most Easy (DC 10) DCs, and be cautious not to set the target DC too high unless you expect most PCs to fail the roll. You'll notice that many DCs in this adventure are set lower than DC 15; that's to provide challenge for 1st level PCs without making success improbable.

Sometimes a failed skill roll would stop the game cold. If this is the case, don't require a roll at all. Just hand wave it and tell the PCs they succeed.

WHO'S WHO IN PERDITION

CALEDONIA ROUNDHILL

Caledonia Roundhill is the half'in shopkeeper at the heart of this story. Her pap died young working as a servant for Criojo - whipped to death, folks say, but it was never proven - and she was raised by her grandpappy Lucan right in the general store downtown. The old half'in did a good job, and Caledonia has run the general store during the last five years since her grandpappy retired. He passed away two months back. Caledonia hates Criojo and his men. She still sells to them, but she extends no credit and does no favors. She refuses to be bullied.

This makes Criojo furious. She has found her well drying up, her house and store infested by long stick-legged biting insects, the stagecoach carrying her beloved robbed and burned (seven dead, including her fiancé; she assumes it was the Killers of Carcass Creek, although that's never been proven.) Every hardship inflicted upon her has made her angrier and more resolute. She is beautiful and determined, the soft coal of her spirit hardened into diamond by constant pressure, and she is determined to have her revenge. She is in desperate need of allies.

If there are half'in characters amongst the PCs, consider changing Caledonia's name and making her their cousin.

Caledonia Roundhill, half' in shopkeeper: Lvl 1, GRIT 2, DRAW 0, WITS 1, HP 12, Def 11, MDef 12. No weapon.

The sort of things that Caledonia might do:

* Give strangers a discount if they are kind or polite
* Buy strangers drinks if they did something she wanted done
* Cook dinner for people who might be friends
* Order the finest merchandise for people she trusts
* Slowly torture someone who had hurt a person she loved
* Carry a grudge for decades, polishing it with her hatred like it was a precious jewel

ALBERTO CRIOJO

Alberto Criojo is a human widowed cattle baron who can afford to be disliked. He is tall, graying, strong-featured, with a gray leather duster and a black cowboy hat so weather-beaten it almost looks gray as well. He has a hard face with deep lines. The sun has bleached his eyes to a pale, colorless blue. He does not give them impression of being a kind man. His hands are large, raw-boned and strong. You can imagine those hands dispassionately snapping someone's neck.

He likes control: of his herds, of his people, of his children, and of the town. If there is ever any doubt what action Criojo takes, it's the one that puts pressure on someone he doesn't yet own, or one that cruelly twists the knife to remind someone that they live or die at his whim. Nobody defies Criojo. Nobody.

Criojo has a large ranch out west of town named the Victory Ranch. While he has dozens of cowboys working for him, most of those are out on the plains at any given time tending to the herds. That means you can reinforce his bodyguard as needed, but don't feel you need to keep

LOVE ON THE PLAINS

Criojo's sons and daughters are attractive, and you may decide that one of them falls madly, irrationally in love with one of the PCs. If so, make up a personality you think your players will react well to for either Gabriel or Luisa Criojo. The young lover will be willing to break their father's strict rules in order to spend time with the PC. This will certainly draw their father's wrath should he find out (and there are a handful of townsfolk spying for Criojo who will tell him in exchange for a few coins.) The crush may be returned by the PC, may be one-sided, or may be rejected. If returned or one-sided, the son or daughter will be willing to help the PC in whatever they ask. If rejected cruelly, the son or daughter will betray the PCs to their father in order to turn Criojo's wrath against them. Have fun with this.

If Criojo is killed, he will rise again at the next dusk as a unique type of zombie.

track of the actual number of workers required for a ranch that size. Criojo usually sends his cowpokes to handle dirty work that he doesn't want to do himself.

Locally Criojo surrounds himself with his hired gun Steeleye, as well as a gang of up to ten bullies and hired guns. There are other people at his ranch -- his half'in cook Mariposa, his sons and daughters (as many of them as you find interesting, of whichever sex, age 6-22), a few maids -- but while Criojo inspires fear and respect in his employees, he doesn't do so well on loyalty. If a person on the ranch isn't a blood relative or hired to kill, he's less likely to pick up a gun to defend the man.

Criojo has one large barn on his property that he doesn't allow anyone in. It's alongside a specially reinforced corral, and any cattle wrangler will know that animals shun that side of the ranch. It smells like rotting meat. This barn is where Criojo keeps the zombies that he has purchased from the shee. Originally he bought only the corpses of the locals who thwarted or defied him so that he could make them do menial tasks even in death. He expected that they'd have good work picking autumn fruit in orchards, or planting grain and corn come spring. Now as the cattleman's insane anger slowly grows, he plans to use these undead as a fine army with which to dismantle the town he both hates and desires.

Alberto Criojo, human cattle baron: Lvl 4, GRIT 2, DRAW 1, WITS 1, HP 24, Def 15, MDef 15. Improvised melee weapon +6 (1d8+2). Enraged 1/day for 4 rounds, for +3 atk and dmg but -3 WITS.

Undead Alberto Criojo, zombie terror: Lvl 4, GRIT 3, DRAW -2, WITS 3, HP 25, Def 12, MDef 17. Slam +7 (1d8+3). Once per day, one round after being killed springs back to his feet with 10 hit points. *Hardy 2. Undead.*

The sort of things that Criojo might do:

* Let a man who insulted him walk away, then later have him bushwhacked, beaten and dragged behind a horse

* Purchase a business to fire its employees, driving them into the poorhouse, because he felt they had somehow slighted him

* Pay someone sympathetic to discover an enemy's emotional vulnerabilities, just so he could exploit them

* Deny any criminal activity at all, while relying on corrupt lawmen to support him

* Lose his temper only in private, while staying icily cool in public

* Use formal speech in public to make himself look more respectable

* Pay extra for luxury that demonstrates his status

* Intimidate the weak and vulnerable

STEELEYE

Steeleye is a hill folk gunslinger as evil and cruel as the day is long. He hardly ever speaks. His battered old hat and long straggly beard may the first thing people notice, but that's only until they look him in the eyes. Actually, "eye"; in his left eye socket is a blank steel ball bearing. Townsfolk swear that it's been enchanted by dark magic to make him shoot straight and see in the dark. That may or may not be true, but it's well known that Steeleye is tough as nails and a deadly duelist. He's shot down nine men who have tried to kill Criojo, and that's only the ones people know about.

While Criojo isn't much of a personal combatant while alive, Steeleye does all of his dirty work. He is incorruptible - well,

more accurate to say that he's already utterly corrupt - and irredeemable.

When Steeleye is finally gunned down, the ball bearing will roll out of his eye and end up near the feet of whoever

Western movies are full of stereotypes. This adventure is, too; they're an easy way for your players to get a handle on who's who when there's a whole range of NPCs. In this adventure, some of these roles include:

The Kindly Shopkeeper (and rebellious victim): Caledonia Roundhill

The Cruel Cattleman: Alberto Criojo

The Love Interest: Criojo's son or daughter, as needed

The Deadly Gunslinger: Steeleye

The Devil Itself: Seven Bright Flames

The Threat in the Night: The zombies of local citizens

The Falsely Accused: Brig Olaffson

The Unpredictable Ally: Two Red Horses

The Fallen Sheriff: Sheriff Elijah Carter

The Fiery Preacher: Amanda Cole

The Corrupt Mayor: Mayor Reginald Johnson

The Cheating Gambler: Hank Hitchins

The Crazy Old Coot: Whelkington

The Reluctant Foe: The Haqat tribe of shee

The Cannon Fodder: The Killers of Carcass Creek, and Criojo's cowpokes

That's a lot of folks. Toss the ones you don't want to deal with, or minimize their roles, or bring them in later when it seems useful. If it seems fun, play around with the stereotypes. What if the sheriff is actually the one who's corrupt, not the mayor? As long as you're consistent, change things around as much as you like.

And as always, while stereotypes are great tools for fast character descriptions, stay away from racism and sexism. That's about as far from fun as you can get

---

killed him. It's up to you whether or not it's actually magic.

Steeleye, hill folk gunslinger: Lvl 4, GRIT 2, DRAW 3, WITS -1, HP 24, Def 17, MDef 13. Throwing knife +6 (1d4+2); two .45-cal revolvers +5/+5 (or only one at +7) (2d6+3 each, range 0-2). For one attack per day (decided whenever you like), gain +2 to hit due to his evil eye.

The sort of things that Steeleye might do:

* Gun down a man, light a cigar, then casually step on the body

* Wheeze through his long gray beard instead of speaking

* Stare at someone with the ball bearing in his eye socket, as if it were a real eye

* Scare someone by appearing out of the darkness where he could gun down a

victim, letting the man see him, and then disappearing back into the night

* Kill anyone who betrayed Criojo - his enemies, his preacher, his children, his employees, anyone

* Give up his own life for Criojo

SEVEN BRIGHT FLAMES

Seven Bright Flames is impossibly old and has been the shaman of a native shee tribe for four generations. She's a good person corrupted by evil spirits. For a century her tribe, the Haqat, flourished under her leadership. Seven Bright Flames' increasingly erratic behavior over the past decade is causing divisiveness, rebelliousness, and fear within the Haqat. Recent cruelty has exacerbated this rift.

Her tribe believes it to be senility. The truth is far worse: Seven Bright Flames has a demon living inside of her that extends her life span. Its whispers encourage the shaman to raise undead, conjuring demons from Carcass Creek and placing them into corpses to create zombies. Each ritual she performs makes the demon that much stronger. The demon will grow in power even more as each zombie is eventually destroyed.

Close to insane, the shee part of Seven Bright Flames yearns to finally die; the clever demon within her keeps her alive, waiting until the day that it is powerful enough to completely devour her soul and wear her skin like a suit. The demon is an evil thing, and if Seven Bright Flames had enough free will to do so she would regret the bargain she made 60 years ago.

Although she doesn't look like her true 130 years, the shaman is aged and has become far more physically feeble than most shamans. Her magic rituals are still strong, however, and most of her tribe will defend her with their own

lives unless they're convinced that she has become irreversibly corrupt.

Seven Bright Flames, shee shaman: Lvl 5, GRIT -2, DRAW -2, WITS 4, HP 24, Def 13, MDef 19. No weapon attacks. Power attack bonus +9 (signature spirit powers are marked): *minor flame spirit* (1d6+5 dmg), *spirit veil*, *angering the spirits of iron*, *curse of vermin*, *call forth the dead voice*.

The sort of things the corrupted Seven Bright Flames might do:

* Betray anyone not of her own tribe, if it meant bettering her or her tribe's condition

* Make bargains with bad people, even knowing that her tribe would object, if she planned to betray them later

* Exile a tribe member who challenged her authority or wisdom, declaring contact with the rebel to be taboo

* Flay an enemy for enjoyment, or as an example to others

* Bring a prisoner's corpse to Carcass Creek at midnight, so as to summon a new demon into it and turn it into a zombie

* Bargain away her own soul to live forever

BRIG OLAFFSON

He's not smart, and he's not worldly, but he's a hard worker and a good son. When his father Olaf Thiggunson decided to buy some zombies from Hank Hitchins, Brig didn't approve but it wasn't his place to say anything. Olaf was right; the old dead bandits were good workers, and it was like they were punishing 'em for being outlaws by making them work 24 hours a day in the mine. And sure, the clan's gold output has pretty much doubled since then, and extra coin helps salve a guilty conscience. Brig knows that using the dead folks as slaves (or really, for anything) is wrong, but he's a hill folk, so maybe he can be excused for a certain amount of greed. He's sworn to keep his clan's secret, and he's done a good job.

But now Brig saw Hank Hitchins murder someone in cold blood, and then Hitchins turned the gun towards Brig in an attempt to get rid of witnesses. Brig ran. His father Olaf is furious that they now have a murderer stalking them, so the clan has taken the traditional hill folk way out. They've holed up, taking refuge in their mine until this whole thing blows over. Anyone who wants Brig is going to have to come in and take him, and that's tougher than it seems.

Thing is, the hill folk don't know that Brig is wanted for murder. They just think Hitchins may be coming to kill him, and it hasn't even occurred to them that the law might come instead. That means they've set up lethal traps, and they're going to be awfully surprised when someone explains the truth. There may be a lot of dead hill folk by the time that happens... if it happens at all.

Brig Olaffson, hill folk miner: Lvl 1, GRIT 4, DRAW 0, WITS 0, HP 14, Def 11, MDef 11. Hatchet +5 melee (1d6+4) or +1 thrown (1d6, range 0).

The sort of things Brig Olaffson might do:

* Work a friend's shift in the mine if they weren't feeling too well

* Drive a fair but hard bargain with shopkeepers in town

* Tell the truth, even if it made him look bad

* Run from a fight unless a loved one was at stake

TWO RED HORSES

This young shee was once considered by the Haqat to be the best of her generation. She is brave, smart, and wise. She is also the only Haqat who has been willing to denounce Seven Bright Flames' growing cruelty. In punishment she has been banished from her tribe and declared taboo. Any member of the Haqat that has interaction with her is marked for ritual death, as is their custom. Two Red Horses knows this and stays away from her tribesmembers. She is self-reliant but lonely and bitter.

Two Red Horses is a wild card who lives outside of Perdition, and she can appear mysteriously to help or hinder the PCs. If following the PCs to learn more about their intentions, as she sometimes does with groups of strangers to the area who look dangerous, she will use her camouflage skills and her long bow with great effect. Against the Killers of Carcass Creek, zombies, or an ambush by Criojo's men, Two Red Horses may choose to warn the PCs or help kill their foes. Against members of the Haqat, including Seven Bright Flames herself, she will shoot at the PCs or attempt to warn them off. Her loyalties clash between what she knows is right and her love for her forbidden tribe, and she remains suspicious of anyone who tries to provide an easy answer.

Two Red Horses, shee scout: Lvl 2, GRIT 2, DRAW 1, WITS 2, HP 16, Def 13, MDef 14. Hatchet +3 (1d6+2); long bow +3 or +4 at range 3 or more (1d6+1). Wilderness skill +6.

The sort of things Two Red Horses might do:

* Silently leave a slain coyote by the campfire of men who don't know how to hunt

* Avenge wrongdoing so long as she could not be caught or easily identified

* Obey her shaman's command to leave her tribe, although she knows the shaman has become corrupt

* Lend a hand to the PCs if they seem to have gotten over their heads

* Stay silent about her secrets, even under torture, until someone has shown themselves worthy of her trust

SHERIFF ELIJAH CARTER

Carter was a damned good sheriff before Hank Hitchins brought him a bottle of good whiskey last year as a thank you gift. Understandably, Carter drank it - and then Hitchins told him that it had been cursed and poisoned by a shee shaman. Continue to drink the bottles of whiskey Hitchins would supply, and the sheriff would be fine. Stop, and the sheriff would die hideously, puking up his own intestines in the dusty street, within three days.

Of course, the sheriff didn't believe him and threw the huckster in jail. 12 hours later, feverishly sweating and vomiting and sure he was about to die, the sheriff begged Hitchins for a cure. Hitchins laid down the law: the sheriff was to turn a blind eye to anything that he or Alberto Criojo did in Perdition, and the sheriff could stay alive. Stand up for himself or talk back, and the supply of ensorcelled whiskey would be completely cut off. A few hours later, hallucinating and in mortal pain, the sheriff agreed.

Since then Hitchins has supplied the sheriff with about a bottle of whiskey a day, and he no longer has to urge the sheriff to drink. Sheriff Carter is still a good man at heart but he's sunk in a morass of guilt, shame, and alcoholism. He's never learned that Hitchins lied; there's no ensorcelled whiskey. He'd just used his mentalist powers along with a rare desert plant that poisoned that first bottle and a few bottles after that. By now, it's the sheriff's own imagination that does the rest.

So the deputies have quit in disgust, the sheriff spends most of his time insensible, and Criojo's ranch hands have more or less free rein in town. The sheriff's last deputy was killed in a duel with Steeleye last month. The sheriff hasn't dared arrest Steeleye for murder.

There's still a good man in there behind the alcohol. It's possible through role-playing that the PCs can befriend the sheriff, sober him up, and steady him through the time he'll need to recover. If they try, he'll likely make them deputies. If they don't, and they oppose Criojo's interests, he'll be forced to try and arrest them.

Sheriff Elijah Carter, human marshal: Lvl 3, GRIT 1, DRAW 1, WITS 0, HP 19, Def 16, MDef 15. Fist +4 (1d3+1);

.38-cal revolver +5 (1d6+1). Can heal 3 people 6 HP each by sharing a drink. Currently unable to detect bad intent, as his WITS of 1 is lowered by alcohol.

The sort of things Sheriff Carter might do:

* Stumble drunkenly into the saloon, gun drawn, to arrest the PCs on Criojo's orders

* Be kind to people in jail, knowing that they didn't deserve to be arrested

* Treat mocking and laughter as another reason to down his "cursed" whiskey

* Threaten to shoot anyone reaching for his bottle, in an attempt to save their life too

* Show no sign of hope until someone kind convinces him that his problem can be solved

* If sober, bravely sacrifice his own life to save a friend who had helped him

PREACHER AMANDA COLE

The preacher is an older woman with a fiery temperament and an iron will. She is the shepherd of the All-Mighty in Perdition and she takes her job seriously. She's known for ranting against the evil of drink - she and Sheriff Carter were once lovers, and her inability to stop his slide into alcoholism has broken her heart - and she cleaves to what she believes is right no matter what danger it brings her. Criojo and his men have anonymously tried to corrupt her many times, and she has remained resolute.

This means she's also stubborn as a rattlesnake. She doesn't believe in disinterring buried coffins unless she's convinced beyond a shadow of a doubt that it's essential. She worries that disturbing

remains may make it hard for people to reach paradise. If she is convinced that bodies have been robbed from or stolen, however, she may be able to be swayed.

Amanda Cole, human preacher: Lvl 3, GRIT 0, DRAW 0, WITS 3, HP 18, Def 13, MDef 16. Staff +3 (1d4+1),

Rebuke +6 vs MDef (1d6); prayers +6 (signature prayers are marked): *Arise, Bless, Inspire, Rebuke Undead, Stop Bleeding.* Amity skill +7.

The sort of things Amanda Cole might do:

* Forbid (at least initially) the excavation of a grave, just because someone suspected a crime they couldn't prove
* Allow the excavation of a grave if she was convinced that someone's immortal soul was at stake
* Lead her congregation in prayer to condemn (or perhaps support if she thinks they're doing the All-Mighty's work) the actions of the PCs, thus using her considerable sway around town to hinder or help the PCs' actions
* Loudly condemn other townsfolk she feels are corrupt, such as the mayor, Alberto Criojo, or the "Godless savage" shee tribe of the Haqat
* Offer unconditional support to anyone who tries to save the sheriff from his own drunkenness

MAYOR REGINALD JOHNSON

The mayor is a dapper little man. He wears a black bowler hat, weighs 130 lbs soaking wet, has an impeccably trimmed mustache, and is detail-oriented and risk-averse enough to be good at running the town of Perdition. He's also an inveterate coward who has been firmly cowed by Criojo's threats. He would fold up before a strong wind, never mind a serious threat. Alberto Criojo values that in an elected official.

Mayor Reginald Johnson, human bureaucrat: Lvl 1, GRIT -1, DRAW 1, WITS 3, HP 9, Def 12, MDef 14. No weapon.

The sort of things Mayor Johnson might do:

* Publicly welcome the PCs after they defeated local outlaws
* Confess, in panic, upon being threatened by someone particularly intimidating
* Bargain for his life, his reputation or his job
* Throw his support behind a likely victor
* Publicly fret about the local shee tribe the Haqat, but not take any action against them
* Hypocritically try to appease everyone, so that whoever's on top at the end of the day thinks he's a friend

HANK HITCHINS

Hitchins is a mentalist from out east, a fast-talking quick-smiling son-of-a-bitch huckster with a soul of ice and a talent for making folks like him. Not many people know he's a mentalist. He owns the local stagecoach company, Hitchins Stage and Freight. It provides transportation to and from nearby towns, and Hitchins often arranges for armed riders to accompany it. The only stagecoach attacked by the Killers of Carcass Creek turned out to be the one that Caledonia Roundhill's fiancé was on. Darned shame. Hitchins is popular in town and lives large; he drinks, gambles (quite well, in fact, since he uses magic to cheat), tips large and laughs often. He's known as a source for people who need things but don't want to go through the General Store for them. If someone wants something smuggled into or out of town, whether it's a mail order engagement ring or a parcel of rare drugs, they go through Hitchins.

Hank Hitchins, human mentalist: Lvl 4, GRIT -1, DRAW 2, WITS 2, HP 21, Def 16, MDef 16. .32-cal pistol +6 (1d6); mentalist trick +6 (signature tricks are marked): *Charm Person, Hypnotism, Silent Illusion, ESP, Sixth Sense*. Wile skill +8.

The sort of things Hitchins might do:

* Buy a round of drinks for the house

* Never turn down an invitation to gamble

* Ask the PCs to provide protection for a stagecoach carrying hill folk gold to a larger bank

* Grab a beautiful girl and dance on a table to his favorite song

* Always dress formally, with never a hair or whisker out of place

* Accept sleazy and unethical business because it made him money

* Kick a dog to death if no one was watching, or give the dog a friendly pat if they were

* Cheat at gambling, possibly by using ESP

* Pay well for illegal services in order to ensure silence

* Tie off loose ends so that he's never caught in a lie

WHELKINGTON

Joe Whelkington is the elderly town coffin maker and gravedigger. He is rail skinny, wildly bearded, balding, and usually drunk. It's sure possible that he's a bit crazy, and he speaks in authentic frontier gibberish. He knows about the grave robbing, of course, since he was the one that made it possible. He's been paid good dollars for every corpse turned over to Hank Hitchins.

He's spent almost none of this blood money, as owning it consumes him with guilt. What if he spent it and someone asked where it came from? All $220 of it is stored in a pine coffin at the bottom of a pile in Whelkington's workshop.

The PCs are bound to question him if they suspect grave robbing. His unintelligible mumbling might protect him for a minute, and he can honestly say that he never took an item off of a dead body, but he's bound to break quickly. Hitchins may have to eliminate him early if he thinks Whelkington might confess their little secret.

Whelkington, human gravedigger: Lvl 1, GRIT 1, DRAW -1, WITS -1, HP 1 (cowpoke), Def 10, MDef 10. No attacks.

The sort of things Whelkington might do:

* Mumble unintelligibly

* Have a few graves pre-dug in case he's drunk on a day a few folks get shot

* Measure a live person for their coffin as soon as he hears they're goin' up against Steeleye

* Act friendly with Hank Hitchins, but leave guiltily as soon as anyone notices or walks nearby

* Sleep in a coffin or sneak into an empty hotel room over at The Majestic when he's too drunk to find his bed

* Bathe once a month whether he needs it or not

* Steal corpses from coffins and replace them with rocks, just so he can sell the bodies to Hank Hitchins in exchange for cash he's too scared to actually spend

CHAPTER FOURTEEN
PROLOGUE

SUMMARY

On their way into the town of Perdition, the PCs are attacked by a few murderous outlaws known as the Killers of Carcass Creek. The outlaws are well equipped with gear, some of which is marked as coming from the local general store in Perdition. The PCs kill some, perhaps chase others off, and possibly follow them back to the rest of their gang in a protected box canyon north of Carcass Creek.

SETUP

It's up to you and your group why they're headed towards Perdition.

Maybe they need to meet, shoot, arrest or give a message to someone who lives there. Maybe they've received a letter from Caledonia Roundhill asking for help, or one of the PCs is related to the troubled sheriff. This is a great way for you to inform the PCs about Perdition ahead of time. Consider giving everyone one person in town that they know or have heard of.

If you're using this adventure to introduce *Owl Hoot Trail* to your players, start the heroes *in media res* on their way to Perdition. The town lies in the western foothills of a tall, jagged mountain range

HOW MUCH FANTASY DO YOU WANT IN YOUR WESTERN?

Owl Hoot Trail is a game which mixes fantasy and a little horror with classic Western themes. This adventure is written in a way that assumes Perdition is a standard dusty little western town; it's heavy on cowboys and light on fantasy. This doesn't have to be the case. If you and your players want, crank up the fantasy quotient to make Criojo a real baron, and include owlbear herds, vampiric tumbleweed, mentalists dueling gunslingers, and even free-range pegasi. If you decide Alberto Criojo has paid a crazy old gadgeteer to construct him a giant mechanical battle engine, it's only going to make the game more interesting.

known as The Harpies, right on the edge of the near-endless plains. The PCs will be headed west towards Perdition and they'll have just come through a snow-filled mountain pass. When the game starts the PCs are probably tired, filthy, cold, and ready for a hot bath and a strong drink.

If this isn't the first adventure for the heroes, set Perdition wherever you please. All you need is a set of hills for the hill folk and Carcass Creek, and a set of good cattle grazing plains for Alberto Criojo. Everything else can be moved or changed without consequence.

PROLOGUE SCENE I
OUTLAW AMBUSH
(MODERATE CHALLENGE)

Three of the least competent members of the Killers of Carcass Creek have decided to earn a little extra money by striking out on their own. In an attempt to make some easy cash and gain some reputation, Chet and his two unnamed associates have set up a small ambush near the mountain pass east of Perdition. The outlaws expect to walk away from this fight with money and respect. They're going to be disappointed.

With one outlaw hidden up on a rock outcropping behind boulders, Chet and the other outlaw will (over)confidently ride out from cover and confront the PCs, voluntarily giving up any chance of Surprise. Chet will brag and bluster, announcing they're with the Killers of Carcass Creek and demanding the PCs lay down their weapons, supplies, and hand over their horses. He expects fear to do the rest, and anticipates that anyone who has ever heard of them will gladly volunteer their valuables. Unfortunately, the PCs have probably never heard of the gang, which will catch Chet off-guard.

None of these three men have ever been seriously hurt before. They are followers instead of leaders, and they may be out-numbered. Chet will flee if he is wounded to half his HP without being killed. In addition, as soon as Chet goes down the other two will make a break for it and ride like hell for two hours back to Hangman's Gulch, the hidden box canyon that the Killers of Carcass Creek use as a hideout. It's quite likely that the PCs will kill them before they succeed in escaping. If taken captive and questioned, any of the outlaws can give the following information:

* They're new members of the Killers of Carcass Creek. The others give them menial jobs and don't particularly respect them, so it was Chet's idea for the three outlaws to do a little robbing on their own.

* There are 8 other members of the gang. The leader of the Killers is a shee gunman named One Bloody

---

This fight is meant to be easy. The outlaws are overconfident and inexperienced, so this is a good chance for the players to learn the rules. Have fun with this and give them chances to try different tactics. Examples might include an Amity + WITS check to convince them that the PCs want to sign up for their gang, a Wile + GRIT roll to intimidate them, a Wilderness + DRAW roll to pull Chet down off his horse, and so forth.

Knife. He's the best outlaw in the bunch, but he's a little crazy. He takes great pleasure in killing and he prefers to use a blade. These three outlaws *really* don't want to get on One Bloody Knife's bad side.

* There's a small reward posted down in Perdition for each of these three - $50 alive, $25 dead - but One Bloody Knife will bring in $500 dead or alive. Last these three checked, the reward for wiping out all 11 members of the gang was a flat $2000.

Each outlaw has about $5, some food supplies, a Hamilton Improved Double-Action .32-cal revolver, some ammo, and a poorly fed horse. Labeling on the bags of food show that it was purchased in Perdition at the General Store. Should the PCs think to ask the General Store owner Caledonia Roundhill about this later, she will state that no outlaw shops at her store. (This is true. The stagecoach owner Hank Hitchins has been supplying the gang of outlaws and regularly smuggles them food out of Perdition.)

If an interrogation is well role-played (or if you prefer, on a Normal (DC 15) Wile + GRIT intimidation roll), the terrified outlaws can give accurate directions to Hangman's Gulch. If the interrogation isn't impressive, they will instead give directions to a ghost cave where an old prospector's spectre tries to kill all that enter.

Chet, Killer of Carcass Creek, human gunslinger: Lvl 2, GRIT 1, DRAW 2, WITS 0, HP 15, Def 14, MDef 11. One .32-cal revolver +3 (1d6+1 dmg, range 0-1).

2 Unnamed Killers of Carcass Creek, human gunslingers: Lvl 1, GRIT 1, DRAW 2, WITS 0, HP 1 (cowpoke), Def 13, MDef 11. .32-cal revolver +3 (1d6+1 dmg, range 0-1) or .32-cal rifle +3 (1d6+3 dmg, range 2-3).

SCENE CONCLUSION

This scene concludes when the PCs have killed Chet and his cohorts, taken them into custody, or allowed them to escape. From here they may keep heading for Perdition, head to the ghost cave thinking it's the outlaw hideout, or

---

The eight other members of the Killers of Carcass Creek:

* One Bloody Knife, shee ruffian, a savage knife fighter who's unpredictable and probably insane
* Octavius Runcible, human gadgeteer, a crazed inventor of deadly devices
* Dead Shot Sheila, human gunslinger, an impatient bank robber with an itchy trigger finger
* Stumpy One-gun, half'in scout, ornery cook and inadvertent comic relief
* Four nameless extras of no particular fame, who you should feel free to develop further

actually head for Hangman's Gulch to try and take out the Killers of Carcass Creek.

If the PCs bring the bodies into town, they'll get their reward from the inebriated sheriff. If they leave the bodies alongside the trail, Whelkington will eventually ride out for the corpses. Either way, these three may end up reanimated as zombies and sold to Criojo a few days later.

WHAT COULD GO WRONG?

If the PCs get wiped out - unlikely but possible with a lucky shot or two - they'll learn that even incompetent men with guns can be deadly. You may decide that Two Red Horses is watching this confrontation from afar. If so, she may mysteriously help the PCs with a few well-placed arrows from her long bow.

If all the bandits are killed, or the PCs don't think (or care) to ask about their hideout, that's fine. The Killers of Carcass Creek, now with eight members, will continue to plague travelers in and out of Perdition until the PCs or someone else decide to deal with them. You should use them selectively to add tension, create drama, or add trouble whenever the game threatens to slow down.

PROLOGUE SCENE II PROSPECTOR'S HAUNT

(HARD CHALLENGE)

This encounter only occurs if the PCs have been fed false information by Chet and his outlaws about the location of Hangman's Gulch.

Prospector's Haunt is in the foothills about an hour west from where Chet

and his friends tried to rob the PCs. It'll be obvious to any PC by making an Easy (DC 10) Wilderness + WITS roll that the path to this cave isn't frequented by horses or a great many people. It'll also be obvious that most of the tracks are leading in, and there are precious few tracks leading out. Suspecting a trap would be both reasonable and accurate.

The twisting mine shaft is carved horizontally into a cliff face about 20' up a steep hillside from the rocky trail. It takes a few minutes to scramble over boulders and climb up to it. These passages were all dug by hand. The sunbaked old prospector who mined them spent over thirty years of his life digging here, convinced that he was finally going to hit the mother lode. When he did, the fierce joy of success gave him a massive heart attack and he dropped dead on the spot. Now his bitter spirit haunts this cave, keeping out anyone who would try to steal his gold.

Spectre: Lvl 4, GRIT 3, DRAW 2, WITS 1, HP 34, Def 16, MDef 15. Soul-suck +7 vs MDef (1d8). Cannot be harmed by normal weapons. *Undead*.

There is no tactical map for this encounter, as Western movies seldom have cautious dungeon crawls through tunnels. Instead, they have cramped shots of actors squeezing through narrow passages, close-ups on sweating brows as they realize that they're in over their heads. Do the same with your PCs. Describe hand-carved and awkwardly shaped passages through the rock, spots where they have to crawl, a long-removed vein of what may have been gold. The PCs don't really need to keep track of the way out; that will be obvious to their characters. It's more important that you make the players feel claustrophobic as they move through these tunnels.

The ghostly prospector will play cat and mouse with anyone who enters the narrow passages, dodging through walls to attack before dodging away. Normal weapons can't hurt him, so this could be a death trap for unprepared PCs. He will allow anyone fleeing to successfully escape. Be sure to allow this; if you don't, this becomes a Deadly Challenge and he could potentially kill everyone in the group.

Preachers can hold undead at bay with *rebuke undead*. This power will begin to weaken and fail after a few minutes of use, plenty of time to get the group out. If they use *rebuke undead* to get the group farther into the mine, it should fail at the most cinematic minute, with a round or two of gradual warning.

In the deepest part of the mine, eight zones into the tunnels, the prospector's fantastic discovery can be found. The old man's skeleton lies directly in front of a nugget of gold the size of a baby's fist. It's worth at least $3000, maybe more in a larger city. Removing the nugget will require another eight hours of mining work to remove the rock remaining around the nugget. Another $500 of small gold nuggets remains in the rotting pockets of the dead prospector's pants.

The prospector's ghost can be permanently put to rest by telling him that his claim will be registered or deposited at the bank in his name, and then actually doing so. This will allow his spirit to sleep easily. Telling him that his claim will be honored, and then not honoring it, will likely result in an unpleasant haunting at some inconvenient time in the future.

These tunnels could be developed into a working and profitable mine if you have any interest in allowing it. If not, this nugget is the last worthwhile chunk of gold in the mine.

SCENE CONCLUSION

This scene concludes when the PCs have turned away with the mine shaft unexplored, have run away unable to defeat the spectre, or have defeated the spectre and have departed (whether or not they found the massive nugget of gold.)

WHAT COULD GO WRONG?

Mining this claim themselves isn't the sort of thing that most adventuring groups will want to do (and if you allow it, have fun with it!) The largest concern is a group who can't hurt the spectre but who refuse to retreat. Be sure to emphasize how normal weapons have absolutely no effect on the ghost; it'll take a gadgeteer, a mentalist, a preacher or a shaman to actually hurt him. This encounter can be truly scary if there's no preacher in the group, so you're encouraged to play this terror up. If any member of the group tries to retreat out of the mine, allow it.

PROLOGUE SCENE III HANGMAN'S GULCH

SENTRY ROCK (MODERATE CHALLENGE)

It takes a Normal (DC 15) Wilderness + WITS check for the PCs to find the winding trail to Hangman's Gulch, unless the PCs were given instructions by the outlaws or you want them to be able to find it. Either way, when they get close the lightly dozing sentry will wake up and spot them unless the person out in front makes a Normal (DC 13) Wile + DRAW roll. This roll alerts the PCs that they may be nearing the hideout. They'll still be automatically spotted if they then proceed without attempting stealth or if they fire a weapon. If they attempt stealth and are taking their time, the difficulty of the Wile + DRAW stealth roll is the scout's Mental Defense, DC 11.

Seeing the napping sentry up on a tall jumble of boulders is almost impossible from the trail. He has near complete cover, boosting his Def by +5. A Normal (DC 15) Wilderness + WITS roll will let a PC hear him gently snoring.

There are chalk marks on the wall here, 35 of them in all. Each chalk mark represents someone shot down by the outlaw gang. The PCs shouldn't have any qualms about punishing them for their crimes.

Unnamed Killer of Carcass Creek, human gunslinger: Lvl 1, GRIT 1, DRAW 2, WITS 0, HP 1 (cowpoke), Def 13, MDef 11. .32-cal revolver +3 (1d6+1 dmg, range 0-1) or .32-cal rifle +3 (1d6+3 dmg, range 2-3).

INSIDE THE BOX CANYON (DEADLY CHALLENGE)

The Killers of Carcass Creek have a superb defensive set-up: three log buildings (one a bunkhouse, one a mess house, and one a saloon), a defensive barricade, a corral for the horses, and an outhouse. A natural spring dribbling down the canyon's back wall provides fresh water.

Hangman's Gulch is a death trap for someone to try and shoot their way into if the defenders are prepared, and make sure your players realize this. The path in has high narrow cliffs on either side, there's a killing field 3 zones long between

the canyon entrance and the defensive barricades, and there's plenty of near complete cover for the defenders with loopholes to shoot through. Someone trying to charge in shooting will be at -5 to hit a defender, plus range penalties, while the defenders will be able to use rifles to easily see and fire upon the attackers.

This changes at night or if the defenders are unprepared for attack. Due to the sentry, the entrance isn't normally watched by the gang members, and most of the time that they aren't out robbing the Killers of Carcass Creek are drunk or carousing. That makes it much easier for a careful group of vigilantes to sneak in and pick them off one by one. Clever players could also climb the canyon walls with a Normal (DC 13) Wilderness + DRAW skill check and start an avalanche, poison the water supply, or any other sneaky gambit that gives them an advantage. Give the characters' Wile + DRAW stealth rolls a +2 to +4 bonus against the outlaws' Mental Defenses, depending on how distracted or inebriated the outlaws are.

The eight surviving members of the Killers of Carcass Creek are:

One Bloody Knife, shee ruffian, a savage knife fighter: Lvl 3, GRIT 3, DRAW 1, WITS 0, HP 21, Def 14, MDef 13. Dirty Fighting (with hunting knife) +6 (1d8+3). Enraged 1/day for 3 rounds, for +3 atk and dmg but -3 WITS.

Octavius Runcible, human gadgeteer, a crazed inventor of deadly devices: Lvl 2, GRIT -1, DRAW 1, WITS 3, HP 13, Def 13, MDef 15. Powers +5 (signature gadgets are marked): *Energon Projector, Phosphorescence Agitator, Deflector Coil, Crank-operated Electroprod.*

Dead Shot Sheila, human gunslinger, an impatient bank robber with an itchy trigger finger: Lvl 2. GRIT 1, DRAW 2, WITS 0, HP 12, Def 13, MDef 12. .41-cal pistol +4 or +2/+2 (2d4+1, range 0-1).

Stumpy One-gun, half'in scout, ornery cook and comic relief: Lvl 2, GRIT 2, DRAW 1, WITS 1, HP 13, Def 14, MDef 13. .45-cal revolver (which he can barely hold) +3 (2d6, range 0-2).

The other three members of the gang can be customized by you. If that isn't desired or necessary, they're nameless extras doomed to die with the following stats:

3 Unnamed Killers of Carcass Creek, human gunslinger: Lvl 1, GRIT 1, DRAW 2, WITS 0, HP 1 (cowpoke), Def 13, MDef 11. .32-cal revolver +3 (1d6+1 dmg, range 0-1) or .32-cal rifle +3 (1d6+3 dmg, range 2-3).

If any of the gang are captured and interrogated, they can recount how they're regularly supplied by someone in Perdition, although they've never learned who. Money is left behind a particular rock; supplies get left at the same rock a few days later. The Killers believe that someone wants them producing a whole lot of corpses, as there's always extra ammo, but they don't know who or why. They don't particularly care, either. They aren't very bright, just violent and greedy.

The Killers have drunk or whored away most of the money they've stolen, but what's left is in a heavy lockbox in the saloon. One Bloody Knife carries the key around his neck. There's a passel of random jewelry and personal possessions, a few holy books, whatever tools or devices you choose, and $320. That said, a few of the outlaws have nice weapons and horses, and there's a heck of a reward for the capture of the entire gang - an even $2000 for all 11 members.

The Killers also have what's left of their massive haul when they robbed Perdition's bank last month. They've spent more than two thousand dollars ordering the parts for Octavius Runcible's mechanical masterpiece - some sort of "giant mechanical insect" is all he'll say - but there's still $1200 left in the bank's distinctive money bags. The PCs will receive a $500 reward if they return the remaining money to Perdition.

Stuck into the lockbox is an unsigned note that's filthy and slightly ripped. It says "Leave people you shoot up by Carcass Creek. $25 a corpse in cash or supplies. Consider it an incentive." If you want them to, a handful of people back in town can identify this handwriting as that of Hank Hitchins, the stagecoach owner, but most people have never seen his handwriting and will not recognize it. The outlaws don't know why someone is willing to pay them for dead bodies, but they're not exactly smart or curious enough to argue.

SCENE CONCLUSION

This scene concludes when the PCs retreat, when all the Killers are dead or captured or escaped, or when all the PCs are dead or captured.

WHAT COULD GO WRONG?

The worst case scenario is if the PCs alert the sentry then ride into Hangman's Gulch with guns blazing. All seven outlaws, everyone except for the sentry, will be behind the barricades shooting away. It's likely to be a massacre. Feel free to let the PCs try this tactic, but make sure they know it could be a very stylish method of suicide.

If this happens, the Killers will take captive anyone who is left on the ground unconscious. These PCs will be saved and imprisoned by the Killers for possible ransoming and/or later torture by One Bloody Knife. This may give the group a chance for a heroic jailbreak if they are initially defeated. Think cinematically, and give the group a fair chance to free themselves while most of the outlaws are drunkenly celebrating. The outlaws aren't idiots, however, so the PCs should have to come up with a creative plan.

If a few PCs escape, or the entire group withdraws, a few of the Killers will follow them and stalk them through the mountains to stop them from reaching Perdition. One PC (picked before rolling this skill check) will need to make a Normal (DC 15) Wilderness + WITS check to outwit and mislead the gang, or all the PCs will need to make a Normal (DC 13) Wilderness + GRIT check to outdistance their foes. Failure means that the tracking outlaws catch up in a locale of your choice. Choose a number of Killers based on the PCs' health, erring towards fewer.

If any of the outlaws escape, they'll take to the mountains for a time and lie low. They won't be seen again in this adventure unless you decide it would make things more interesting.

PROLOGUE SCENE IV
CARCASS CREEK
(EASY CHALLENGE)

This non-combat scene introduces the PCs to the mystery of Carcass Creek.

As they ride to Perdition, whether or not they have sidetracked to deal with outlaws, their trail will take them along a pleasant little stream that runs beside the path. It will be that much more surprising when they see the boneyard that is the watering hole of Carcass Creek. The stream opens up into 30' diameter rock watering hole, and the clearing is a place of death. Animal skeletons old and new litter the ground here, hundreds of them, several feet deep in places. The water appears clean and fresh, but it's clear that any animal that has drunk from the pond - birds, wolves, rats, cows, horses, anything - has died almost immediately. The vegetation within about 20' of the pond is also dead. Just past this watering hole the vegetation grows again, and there are no skeletons. The problem is only around the pond. Someone has hammered a sign into the ground here; the only thing on the sign is a skull.

Many of the animal skeletons are ripped apart and scattered by predators and scavengers who come here to prey on the freshly dead. At the northern edge of the watering hole, bones have been clearly shoved aside to grant access to the water.

An Easy (DC 10) Wilderness + WITS roll will reveal interesting tracks in this area left in the dried clay. Shee have been here, recently and in significant numbers. They wore handmade shoes. There are marks in the mud where a number of human-sized bodies have been lain down flat. A Normal (DC 15) Wilderness + WITS finds faint signs of dried blood in this area, as well as a single silver dollar that must have fallen from someone's pocket. A Hard (DC 20) check reveals that although it's hard to tell, it looks like more people walked away from this spot than walked into it. There is an area of cracked and hardened clay next to the water that smells slightly of brimstone; preachers and shamans who examine this spot feel uncomfortable.

These tracks were left by the Haqat when Seven Bright Flames reanimated the dead.

The PCs will likely investigate the pool, but there is nothing unusual under its waters. A marshal sensing trouble will get a very bad feeling from the spot. Anyone foolish enough to sip or swim in the water must make a Hard (DC 20) Toughness + GRIT check. Success means they drop to 0 hit points. Failure means that they drop to 0 hit points and suffer an injury. If they flat-out drink the water here in any quantity, the DC rises to Very Hard (DC 25). Water from Carcass Creek can be brought away, however; it reverts to fresh water once it's more than 20' (or one zone) away from the pond. That may surprise someone who thinks to take the water for poisoning an enemy.

CHAPTER FIFTEEN
ACT ONE

SUMMARY

The PCs arrive in the town of Perdition. There they meet the local cattle baron Alberto Criojo and his entourage. They learn Criojo somehow has a pocket watch that should have been buried with the local shopkeeper's late grandfather. When trying to help, they soon discover that the sheriff is a drunken wreck and the mayor is a coward who's been bought and paid for by Criojo.

The half'in shopkeeper tries to hire the PCs to steal back the watch or convince the mayor to give her permission to disinter her grandfather. If she can prove that Criojo somehow stole that watch, she'll have a lever against him. Problem is, you can't just dig up a body. The PCs will have to work hard to sway the mayor and the preacher, and may have to dig up the coffin themselves in secret. They soon learn that the coffin is filled with rocks instead of a corpse, and the body is missing. In fact, many bodies are missing - almost every corpse from the last two years.

While the grave robbing is being discovered, the guilty gravedigger is murdered by the man who'd been paying him to steal bodies. A hill folk miner named Brig Olaffson witnesses the murder and flees before he's shot himself, but most folks assume it's Brig who killed the drunken old gravedigger. A bounty is put on his head and the PCs are asked to go arrest him.

ENTERING PERDITION

The town of Perdition is dusty and dry, nestled in foothills where the wind off the prairies always seem to carry the scent of far-away deserts. Mountains known as the Harpies rise up behind town to the east, blocking the dawn light and making for dim mornings. Carcass Creek wends its way down from the mountains towards larger rivers far away. Not many people live near Perdition, but they're a diverse bunch; that far out from civilization, people tend to watch out for one another. The only native tribe nearby is a tribe of shee known as the Haqat.

There are any number of places the PCs may go when they enter town. Refer to the map and the list of NPCs for information, and make up anyone or any location that isn't already detailed.

When the PCs enter town, they'll likely be coming down the main street from the west. They can head anywhere they like. The sheriff is drunk like normal, but will arrange to pay rewards the next morning.

The goal in this scene is for the PCs to meet the cattle baron Alberto Criojo and his entourage, and to be asked by the shopkeeper Caledonia Roundhill for help in getting her grandfather disinterred. If the PCs don't seem inclined to enter the General Store, have NPCs in other locations ('Ole One Eye's Saloon, the Majestic Hotel, the sheriff's office) mention that Miss Roundhill is looking to hire some freelance help or a hired gun.

The town of Perdition is almost a one-street town. Any location without named NPCs is ideal for you to add your own. Stores and buildings along its one main street include:

* Assayer and Land Office, where property claims are filed and gold is weighed by finicky and bookish clerks.

* The First Bank of Perdition, robbed last month by the Killers of Carcass Creek and still closed for business due to a large hole in the east wall.

* Sarana's Warehouse, run by the gossiping widower Thomas Sarana, where supplies and goods are locked away and stored until needed by businesses in town.

* The Majestic Hotel, an establishment that is anything but. Owned by a human woman named Acacia Bellevue who dreams big, the hotel is full of interesting locals, unoccupied hotel rooms, and any quirky visitors to town you want to include. If an visitor to town is looking to rent themselves some temporary companionship, he or she can probably find a handsome-but-dissolute cowboy or a clever dancing girl by asking here.

* Mayor's Office, run by the cowardly but officious mayor Reginald Johnson.

* The livestock and horse trader Handy Dan's Stables. Dan would be happy to sell the PCs a horse, although all the best horseflesh gets bought by Criojo.

* Longarm Gun Shop, run by an elderly one-armed gunslinger named Cletus with a big mustache and a bad attitude.

* Wooden gallows, where murderers and horse thieves are hanged. They need repair and are poorly maintained.

* Sheriff's Office and Jail, seldom used and run by the constantly drunk sheriff Elijah Carter. Peeling "Wanted" posters line the outside wall.

* General Store & Mining Supplies, run by the fiery half'in storekeeper Caledonia Roundhill.

* Hitchins Stage and Freight, run by the charming but secretly despicable gambler Hank Hitchins. The stagecoach is the best solution for anyone wishing to move freight or ride away from town in comfort.

* Groat the elderly hillfolk Barber, who can offer a bath and a shave despite his shaky hands.

* 'Ole One-Eye's Saloon, full of bullying roustabouts, portly piano-players and always a poker game or two. The orcish bartender Groomsh ("My parents were religious folk, even if they couldn't spell") spends his day spitting into whiskey glasses and polishing them with an old rag. This is where Hank Hitchens is usually found.

* The Coffin Maker's, run by the mostly crazy and entirely unintelligible gravedigger Joe Whelkington. Locals only know him by his last name.

* Church and town graveyard, clean but rustic, run by the resolute and holy preacher Amanda Cole.

ACT ONE SCENE I
THE SHERIFF AND
THE REWARD

If the PCs killed Chet and his fellow outlaws in the Prologue, their first stop in Perdition will likely be sheriff Elijah Carter's jailhouse at the west end of Perdition's main street. There's no one currently in jail, and Carter has no remaining deputies; they've all quit or been shot down by outlaws that Carter was too drunk or ashamed to go after.

Wanted posters are plastered on the outside wall of the sheriff's office and jail. If any of the PCs are outlaws, their poster will be there. There are also posters for everyone in the Killers of Carcass Creek. Reward bounties range from $50 alive / $25 dead to $2000 for all 11 members of the Killers of Carcass Creek.

Carter is drunk when the PCs arrive. If it's morning, he'll be a third into his bottle of whiskey; if it's night, he'll be most of the way through it. He's still cogent, however. He'll tell the PCs to come back the next morning for their reward. PCs may assume Carter has to get it out of the bank, but the bank has been closed for a month ever since the Killers of Carcass Creek rode into town and robbed it. Carter keeps his money in a safe under the floorboards, and doesn't want anyone to know where it is. He'll tell the PCs that they can just pay the Majestic Hotel in the morning for their $10 rooms.

If the PCs are looking for work, Carter will suggest going after the outlaws or talking to Caledonia Roundhill at the General Store. Under no circumstances will he suggest working for Criojo. He hates the son-of-a-bitch, a fact that will be evident if anyone brings the cattleman up in Carter's presence.

As noted under his description, Carter keeps the reason for his alcoholism a secret. He needs a friend and an ally, if the PCs turn out to be it, he'll gladly deputize them. If they work to get him sober and convince him that he's not actually poisoned or cursed, and he comes to trust them, he'll give his life for them.

WHAT COULD GO WRONG?

At the start of the adventure, Carter is washed up and on his last legs. It's all right if the PCs don't like him or never think to help him. Should they actually attack and kill him, the mayor will have to appoint a new sheriff. He'll appoint Hank Hitchins. That's when things in Perdition will get particularly bad.

If Carter has to arrest the PCs for any reason, he'll do the best job he can considering his drunken haze and shaking hands. It's up to the PCs how to respond. Killing the sheriff will turn many people in town against them, although Criojo will extend an employment invitation as soon as he finds out.

ACT ONE SCENE II
CRIOJO'S MEN
(MODERATE CHALLENGE)

This (probably) non-combat scene occurs when the PCs enter the Caledonia Roundhill's General Store in Perdition. There are seven hard-bitten cowboys lounging out front, gossiping and standing around looking tough. At your discretion up to three of them may harass and bully the PCs, as they do any newcomers in town, and the rest will stand around watching but not interfering. Should they do so and get killed for their trouble, their boss Criojo will not be in the least bit concerned. He has ordered his men to behave respectably, and considers their death a proper repayment for disobedience.

If a PC is willing to risk his skills on a likely death, this is a good opportunity to use the Gunfighter Dueling rules. Be sure the player understands that just as in any gunfight, there's going to be a body left on the dusty street and it may well be his. If he wins, though, killing or humiliating any of Criojo's men will quickly establish a reputation in town for the PCs. The townsfolk may consider this an act of very slow suicide, but they'll respect it regardless.

Criojo's cowboys, human ruffians: Lvl 1, GRIT 2, DRAW 2, WITS -1, HP special (Cowpuncher), Def 13, MDef 10. .32-cal revolver +3 (1d6, range 0-1); dirty fighting +3 (1d6+2). Enraged 1/day for 1 round, for +3 melee dmg but -3 WITS. As Cowpunchers, these ruffians die after receiving an injury or being hit twice for any amount of damage.

The horses tied up beside them are some of the finest mounts the PCs will see in town, especially a chestnut stallion with a beautiful silver-trimmed saddle. That horse is named Conquest and belongs to Criojo.

WHAT COULD GO WRONG?

Killing any of Criojo's boys can't turn the cattle baron against the PCs. The biggest risk in this scene is that the bullying cowpokes provoke the PCs, the PCs push back, and a PC gets killed in the resulting fight. Punishing bullies is

a staple of Western films; so long as the players knows that's a possibility, let them respond however they like.

ACT ONE SCENE III MEETING CRIOJO

Inside, the general store is crowded, clean, and a bit dark. During the daytime sunlight streams through large windows set on each wall. The counter is at the south end of the large room. The PCs will overhear an argument when they enter. Read, paraphrase, or reword the following.

A half'in woman is speaking. "Mister Criojo, I have told you. You and your men can shop at my store if you insist, but you get no credit. I make no special orders. I don't particularly want your money, and I don't want anything to do with you. You, sir, are not welcome here." She tries to stay polite but she sounds furious, and she's staring an older human man in the eye.

The man speaks, slowly and deeply. His voice is calm but manages to sound threatening regardless. "Miss Roundhill - it is Miss, isn't it? I was so sorry about your late fiancé - Miss Roundhill, you are no one to tell me what I can and can't have. I take what I want in this town. You should be appreciative that I'm willing to give you money for it."

As the PCs walk forward, he'll stop talking and turn to look at them. The PCs will see a tall man, older, gray haired, well made clothes but clearly weather-beaten: the local cattle baron Alberto Criojo. Standing beside him is his silent bodyguard Steeleye and three of Criojo's men whose arms are loaded down with supplies.

If the PCs have just had a fight and shots were fired, Criojo will ask if they just killed a few of his boys. He'll then ask if his boys tried to bully them. If the answer to both questions is yes, Criojo will nod acceptingly.

Seeing that strangers are in the store, he'll ask the PCs who they are and why they're in his town. He will introduce himself as a local cattleman. He may offer the PCs work if they look competent. Before the role-playing becomes boring, Criojo will pull out a beautiful pocket watch, check the time, throw a bag of money on Caledonia's counter - more than enough to pay for the supplies - smile thinly and stroll out. He and his boys will ride away back to the Victory Ranch.

Caledonia will have stayed silent and furious throughout this conversation, but anyone looking at the shopkeeper will see her face going dead while when Criojo pulls out his pocket watch. She's clearly shocked by something she just saw.

Alberto Criojo, human cattle baron: Lvl 4, GRIT 2, DRAW 1, WITS 1, HP 24, Def 15, MDef 15. Improvised melee weapon +6 (1d8+2). Enraged 1/day for 4 rounds, for +3 atk and dmg but -3 WITS.

Steeleye, hill folk gunslinger: Lvl 4, GRIT 2, DRAW 3, WITS -1, HP 24, Def 17, MDef 13. Throwing knife +6 (1d4+2); two .45-cal revolvers +5/+5 (or only one at +7) (2d6+3, range 0-2 each). For one attack per day (decided whenever you like), gain +2 to hit due to his evil eye.

Criojo's cowboys, human ruffians: Lvl 1, GRIT 2, DRAW 2, WITS -1, HP special (Cowpuncher), Def 13, MDef 10. .32-cal revolver +3 (1d6, range 0-1); dirty fighting +3 (1d6+2). Enraged 1/day for 1 round, for +3 melee dmg but -3 WITS. As Cowpunchers, these ruffians die after receiving an injury or being hit twice for any amount of damage.

WHAT COULD GO WRONG?

The PCs are more likely to help Caledonia if they dislike Criojo, so the best results occur if Criojo comes across as despicable at first sight. The man is cold, officious and controlling; a bad first impression probably won't be too difficult. People in town instantly get out of his way and pay him terrified respect. The PCs will quickly realize that he's a man of importance and power.

Some groups might start a gunfight right there in the shop. Considering Steeleye and the cowpokes, this will probably end with a lot of dead PCs, but if it happens run with it. Anyone killing Steeleye will be a major enemy for Criojo; anyone killing Criojo will be a target if Steeleye survives; and anyone killing both will change the balance of power in town, but will probably have to be arrested for murder by the sheriff.

Ambitious PCs may encourage a gunfighting showdown with Criojo, Steeleye or any of his hired bullies. Criojo doesn't fight himself; that's what he has Steeleye for. He won't have Steeleye fight for any of his men, though. They're nameless and disposable. Criojo would consider this a good test of a PC's skill and mettle.

If Criojo is killed here, he will spontaneously arise as an intelligent zombie that night at dusk. This will change the flow of the adventure considerably, but will be an awful lot of fun for you as the GM.

Some PCs may want to ignore Caledonia Roundhill and accept Criojo's offer of employment. If so, have them ride out to the Victory Ranch the next day and give them work guarding cattle on the plains from random monsters (such as hungry wolves or an injured and wild owlbear.)

Chances are they'll figure out soon enough that Criojo is a bad, bad man. This is almost certain after they investigate his forbidden barn full of zombies.

ACT ONE SCENE IV MEETING CALEDONIA ROUNDHILL

Caledonia tends to like the PCs if they stand up to Criojo or his men. She's an underdog and she needs allies. She'll warn them that showing Criojo any disrespect at all could earn them a very dangerous enemy here in Perdition. If they still show

no signs of fear, she'll grin and promise to buy each of them a drink in the saloon.

She's scared, though, clearly scared. If anyone asks why, she gathers her thoughts for a minute and explains that she just saw the pocket watch Criojo pulled out. It was her grandpappy Lucan's, she's sure of it, and Lucan Roundhill was buried with it after he died two months ago. How did Criojo get it? She isn't sure what that means, because Criojo couldn't be a grave robber - could he? - but maybe now she has a lever against the cattleman. If she's getting along with the PCs, she'll explain to them that Criojo has tried to force her from her farm and out of this store. He doesn't like being denied anything; he takes it personally. Problem is, he pretty much owns the mayor and the town sheriff is a useless drunken wretch, so that makes things hard on her here in Perdition. Her fiancé was killed, her well dried up, her home and store infested with insects. That just makes her more stubborn to keep the store her grandpappy Lucan started all those years ago.

She asks the PCs if she can hire them. She wants proof that Criojo has her family watch. They can do this one of two ways: find some way to steal it from him, difficult at best, or talk the mayor into briefly disinterring Lucan to prove that the watch has been stolen from his corpse. If it has been, that's proof enough for her.

She'll pay them $100 apiece if they prove graverobbing, or $50 apiece if they try but Criojo's watch isn't her family's after all. She's sure it is, though; she got a good look. Criojo is just too important in town for anyone to force him to hand it over without solid evidence.

If they don't want to take this job, she will ask them to go after the Killers of Carcass Creek. Those outlaws robbed the stagecoach her fiancé was on, and shot and killed everyone but Hank Hitchins the driver. They even robbed the local bank last month and stole a lot of people's money. Caledonia owes them a blood debt, and she really wants to have it paid in full. There is a huge reward for exterminating the gang, and she looks to find someone willing to claim it.

Caledonia Roundhill, half'in shopkeeper: Lvl 1, GRIT 2, DRAW 0, WITS 1, HP 12, Def 11, MDef 12. No weapon.

WHAT COULD GO WRONG?

Caledonia's investigation launches the PCs on the adventure, but it's not a problem if they turn her down. Find a different way to draw them into opposition with Criojo, the Killers of Carcass Creek or the Haqat. These paths may let the PCs realize that townsfolk are being reanimated as zombies, which puts them back on track for the adventure.

Some PCs might decide to rob Caledonia and steal her goods. If so, she'll call the law (such as it is) on them, or hire another band of rivals to bring the now-outlaw PCs to justice. Handle this in whatever way is the most fun for you and your players.

ACT ONE SCENE V QUESTIONING THE GRAVEDIGGER
(EASY CHALLENGE)

The first thing most players will think of after learning that Criojo has Caledonia's family watch is that Whelkington the gravedigger stole it. He didn't, ironically, but he's been doing something worse.

Whelkington isn't a good liar but he has a few things going for him: he's elderly, he's not particularly bright, he's usually inebriated, he's known to be hard-working, and he speaks in authentic frontier gibberish that's hard for most people to understand. He's not going to stand up to anyone questioning him, assuming he can stand up at all. The trick here is whether the PCs ask the correct questions. If they ask if he's been stealing from the corpses, he can honestly answer no; he's never taken as much as a coin or a cufflink off of any body put into his care. It's unlikely at this point that they'll ask if he's been up to anything else, but if they do, Whelkington feels so guilty that he might crumble and confess to stealing the entire corpse. Playing on his guilt or clever questioning is the only thing that will crack him.

WHAT COULD GO WRONG?

If the PCs crack Whelkington, they'll possibly know that he's been selling bodies to Hank Hitchins. They won't know anything else because Whelkington has stayed deliberately ignorant of any further facts (such as what Hitchins has been doing with the bodies.)

If this happens, Hitchins' *sixth sense* will alert him and he'll quickly make himself scarce. He'll try to elude the PCs and shoot Whelkington before the gravedigger can testify; Brig Olaffson will see him do so, Brig will run, and the adventure will skip to Act One Scene 11.

Whelkington, human gravedigger: Lvl 1, GRIT 1, DRAW -1, WITS -1, HP 1 (cowpoke), Def 10, MDef 10, no attacks.

ACT ONE SCENE VI CONVINCING THE MAYOR

(EASY CHALLENGE)

The purpose of this non-combat scene is to role-play with Mayor Reginald Johnson, showing the PCs that he's probably been bribed by Criojo.

Mayor Reginald Johnson's office is a lot like the mayor himself: neat, prim, fussy, precise. The Mayor thinks his job here is to deflect the PCs, dismiss their claims, and find a pretext for getting them out of town before they cause trouble. He figures that Criojo doesn't want them around, which means he doesn't want them either. The problem is that he's terrified of personal violence and he's easily bullied.

If the PCs use actual facts and good sense to convince him to exhume Lucan's body, it's going to be difficult. The mayor has Criojo's bribes and threats to keep him firm, and it will take great role-playing or a Hard (DC 18) Amity + WITS or (if they appeal to him as a frontier hero) Amity + GRIT to convince him. Threats of violence work much more effectively. Convincing role-playing or a Normal (DC 13) Wile + GRIT check will get him to reluctantly allow a disinterment, assuming that the Preacher gives her consent.

The PCs could also fool the Mayor, claiming that they work for Criojo and that he wishes this done. The mayor doesn't know any details about what Criojo's been up to, so he'll believe this fairly easily with a Normal (DC 13) Wile + WITS check. Another tactic is quoting laws about bribing or unduly influencing an elected official, which will succeed on a Normal (DC 13) Learning + DRAW check.

If the PCs end up threatening the Mayor to achieve their goals, he'll harbor a grudge. He's unlikely to be brave enough to do much about it, however.

Mayor Reginald Johnson, human bureaucrat: Lvl 1, GRIT -1, DRAW 1, WITS 3, HP 9, Def 12, MDef 14. No weapon.

WHAT COULD GO WRONG?

If the PCs aren't able to intimidate or otherwise convince Mayor Johnson into allowing an exhumation, they're out of legal ways to proceed. They can sneak into the graveyard and exhume the body themselves, appeal to Preacher Amanda Cole for help (and if they're successful she'll exhume the body with or without the Mayor's permission), or try another tack like stealing the watch from Criojo.

ACT ONE SCENE VII CONVINCING THE PREACHER

(MODERATE CHALLENGE)

Amanda Cole is in her early 60s. She's been preacher in this town for 15 years, and she's one of the few incorruptible people around. That said, she's lonely and she doesn't trust most folks; she preaches the word of the All-Mighty each week in her church, but it's hard for people to get close to her. She's stubborn as a mule. She doesn't approve of alcohol since she's seen her one-time love sheriff Elijah Carter slide into the bottle. If the PCs are known to be drinkers, any difficulty on skill checks with her rises by 5. Likewise, if the PCs are trying to help the sheriff, the difficulty of skill checks to gain the preacher's help drop by 5. It's possible that she'll agree to help the PCs if they promise to try and help the sheriff. She'll feel guilty about this compromise afterward, but in her heart she'll know it's the right one.

The group can also gain the Preacher's support by quoting scripture to her that supports the sanctity of the dead and the punishment of the wicked who defile them. This is a Normal (DC 13) Learning + WITS roll.

The preacher doesn't believe in disinterring buried coffins unless she's completely convinced that the burial site has somehow been profaned or interfered with. It's up to the PCs to persuade her through good role-playing or hard evidence that someone has been stealing from the dead. She may try to question Whelkington about this, but he's currently so drunk that even his normal frontier gibberish is hard to distinguish.

Amanda Cole, human preacher: Lvl 3, GRIT 0, DRAW 0, WITS 3, HP 18, Def 13, MDef 16. Staff +3 (1d4+1), *Rebuke* +6 vs MDef (1d6); prayers +6 (signature prayers are marked): *Arise, Bless, Inspire, Rebuke Undead, Stop Bleeding.* Amity skill +7.

WHAT COULD GO WRONG?

If they infuriate the Preacher, she'll absolutely forbid a disinterment. This will require the PCs to secretly dig up the coffin on their own, only to find it full of rocks, or to try stealing the watch from Criojo instead.

ACT ONE SCENE VIII STEALING THE WATCH
(HARD CHALLENGE)

If the PCs decide to go the route of stealing the watch from Criojo, listen to what their plan is and adjust on the fly. They can ride out to Criojo's ranch for an audience with him, although it takes a Normal (DC 13) Amity + GRIT skill check to talk their way through his door; he likes people who are tough but compliant. If they were at all rude to him previously, this becomes a Hard (DC 20) check. He will meet with them in his parlor or out by a cattle corral. His bodyguard Steeleye will never leave his side. As usual, Criojo is supremely confident and commanding, and the PCs will have an opportunity to watch his men jump at his every wish. Should a problem arise, Criojo has up to ten cowpokes on hand; he is not above tying insolent PCs to the back of a horse and dragging them back to town.

Alternatively, the PCs can lure Criojo and Steeleye into town on a pretext and "bump into him" to try and steal the watch. He'll have fewer men with him, and he'll have to be on his best behavior, but he won't hesitate to have the sheriff arrest a PC for theft if the pickpocketing attempt is noticed.

Actually trying to steal the watch from Criojo requires a Hard (DC 20) Wile + DRAW or (if they befriend him) Amity + DRAW check. If they can somehow distract Steeleye from watching his boss every second, this drops to Hard (DC 18) or even Normal (DC 13) if you think the PCs did an excellent job setting up the theft.

If the theft is not immediately noticed by Criojo or Steeleye, it will not be discovered until the PCs have already left the scene.

Once obtained, Caledonia can immediately confirm that the watch belonged to her Grandpappy; his initials are engraved in it. She can use this evidence to browbeat the Mayor and Preacher into exhuming her Grandpappy's corpse to find out if anything else is missing. This settles the adventure back on track for the end of Act One.

Alberto Criojo, human cattle baron: Lvl 4, GRIT 2, DRAW 1, WITS 1, HP 24, Def 15, MDef 15. Improvised melee weapon +6 (1d8+2). Enraged 1/day for 4 rounds, for +3 atk and dmg but -3 WITS.

Steeleye, hill folk gunslinger: Lvl 4, GRIT 2, DRAW 3, WITS -1, HP 24, Def 17, MDef 13. Throwing knife +6 (1d4+2); two .45-cal revolvers +5/+5 (or only one at +7) (2d6+3, range 0-2 each). For one attack per day (decided whenever you like), gain +2 to hit due to his evil eye.

Criojo's cowboys, human ruffians: Lvl 1, GRIT 2, DRAW 2, WITS -1, HP special (Cowpuncher), Def 13, MDef 10. .32-cal revolver +3 (1d6, range 0-1); dirty fighting +3 (1d6+2). Enraged 1/day for 1 round, for +3 melee dmg but -3 WITS. As Cowpunchers, these ruffians die after receiving an injury or being hit twice for any amount of damage.

WHAT COULD GO WRONG?

Actually stealing the watch is high risk because it could get a PC shot, beaten up, or arrested. It will definitely turn Criojo into an enemy once he figures out what happened. No guts no glory, however; even if the PCs fail, they will make Criojo aware that he's on the verge of being discovered, and he will probably have Hank Hitchins murder Whelkington to stop him from talking.

ACT ONE SCENE IX A LIGHT AT CARCASS CREEK
(MODERATE CHALLENGE)

If the PCs are in town the second night after their arrival, a cold green flickering light can be seen shining from the western hills at midnight. Someone will alert the PCs about this fact, probably by running into 'Ole One Eye's Saloon and shouting "The ghost light! It's back!" From town the light looks positively evil, like an aurora brought down to earth and staked screaming into the soil. It's flickering up from the exact location of Carcass Creek, an hour or more's ride away to the west.

Townsfolk can tell the PCs that this is a sign of the devil and it always happens a few days after someone has died. They claim that the devil rises up at Carcass Creek and pulls the souls of the dead down into Hell. No one wants to go find out what it is.

The light is caused by the shee shaman Seven Bright Flames of the Haqat tribe animating the bodies of any dead outlaws who the PCs recently killed, as well as any other casualties that have occurred in the past day. Arthur Hitchins used his freight coach to smuggle out the bodies to the Haqat. The shaman then pulls demons into the corpses.

If the PCs investigate, Carcass Creek will be empty by the time they arrive. There will be fresh tracks along the banks, and faint wisps of green ghostlight still scud along the top of the water. A twisted minor fiend, summoned but not placed within a corpse, abides in the watering hole until dawn. If any of the PCs approach within one zone of the water, it will rise from the surface and attack.

Creek demon: Lvl 3, GRIT 3, DRAW 1, WITS 3, HP 23, Def 14, MDef 16. Claw +6 (1d6+4); spitting cold green hellfire +4 (1d6, range 0-1).

This fiend disappears forever at dawn, returned to the infernal pits by the light of the rising sun. It can not move farther than 1 zone from the watering hole. If forced farther than this, it vanishes back to Hell. It appears as a tortured soul within a cold green fiery shroud. If the demon is slain, escaping necrotic energy causes every bone in the area to rise up and swirl about for a few seconds like rustling leaves.

The PCs can follow the Haqat's horse tracks with a Hard (DC 20) Wilderness + WITS check. This difficulty drops to a Normal (DC 15) check if the PCs have a good source of light or know where they're probably going. The tracks lead around Perdition to Criojo's ranch, then out into the plains and eventually back to the Haqat village. If the PCs are particularly rapid, which is difficult when trying to track in the darkness, they may be able to catch and confront the Haqat before the new zombies are sold to Criojo. Refer to Act Two Scene 8 for details.

You may decide that Two Red Horses is still watching the PCs from a distance. If so, or if the group has befriended her, she may approach and urge peace when confronting the Haqat. If this occurs, the group is free to ignore her or try to befriend her.

WHAT COULD GO WRONG?

The PCs may choose not to ride out into the foothills in the middle of the night. If so, that's just fine.

This scene is meant to remind the PCs that something creepy is happening out at Carcass Creek, but the watering hole of death is far enough away that they're unlikely to run across the Haqat. If the PCs somehow manage to arrive while Seven Bright Flames is summoning fiends to place inside corpses, the shaman will talk to the PCs about what she's been doing. She will not lie. The Haqat are not aggressive but will defend themselves, and if Two Red Horses is still shadowing the PCs she will act to protect her former tribe.

ACT ONE SCENE X DISINTERRING LUCAN'S COFFIN

It doesn't rain much in Perdition, but it's drizzling while the PCs are disinterring the coffin of Caledonia's grandfather.

Perdition has a high child mortality rate; it's up to you whether any teenagers or younger children who have died in town are also missing. Be aware that adding toddler zombies will make the game considerably more horrific for your players. Judge for yourself whether that's a mood you're shooting for, and if it isn't, the bad guys in this adventure have blessedly retained enough morals to only reanimate adults.

No one can find Whelkington, the gravedigger (who is drunk and passed out in the Majestic Hotel, and about to be murdered by Hank Hitchins), so if the PCs don't wish to use a shovel Caledonia Roundhill and the Preacher will do the hard work themselves. Their effort will eventually shame other townsfolk into helping. By the time they get six feet down, there will be a fair crowd gathered to watch.

Caledonia will hold her breath when the coffin is actually opened. She expects to find her grandfather's body robbed of his wedding ring and pocket watch. What she sees instead is a complete surprise. There's no body in the coffin. Lucan is gone. Instead, the coffin is filled with rocks.

The Mayor calls this appalling; the preacher declares it a sacrilege and an abomination. She sends folks out to find where Whelkington has passed out, as he must be able to explain this. Worried, she has men dig up the bodies of anyone shot in the last few days, such as the shallowly buried outlaws that the PCs may have killed on their way into town. Their coffins, too, are filled with rocks. Investigation will eventually reveal that more than 30 bodies from the last two years are missing.

WHAT COULD GO WRONG?

The PCs may choose not to be there when the grave is disinterred. If so, they'll certainly hear about it afterward.

They may be clever enough to find Whelkington in the hotel before Hitchins has a chance to shoot him. If so, one of two things happen; either they manage to sober Whelkington up and easily break him, causing him to confess that he's been selling dead bodies to Hank Hitchins for years; or Hitchins panics, tries to shoot Whelkington dead, and then makes a desperate run for it. Should the latter occur, make sure hidden records in Hitchins' office reveal that he's been smuggling dead bodies to the Haqat for years.

ACT ONE SCENE XI WHELKINGTON DRINKS HIS LAST

(MODERATE CHALLENGE)

Whether or not the PCs are present for the disinterment of Caledonia's grandfather, the few people remaining back in the Majestic Hotel will hear a shot from upstairs and the sound of running feet. Brig Olaffson, one of the hill folk miners who live out of town, will rush down the stairs and leap onto his horse. He'll ride out of town like a shot, leaving in the opposite direction from the church. A minute later Hank Hitchins and a few other guests will come downstairs, declaring that Whelkington has been shot and killed. People put these two facts together and call for the sheriff. The sheriff puts a warrant out for Brig Olaffson's arrest in connection with the murder.

The murder scene is fairly plain. Whelkington was drunk and passed out in a rented hotel bed. Someone kicked open his door, shot him, and ran. People in the Majestic saw Brig Olaffson running from the hotel.

Once folks know about what has been discovered in the graveyard, they'll assume that Brig and Whelkington were somehow in cahoots when it came to stealing bodies. No one has any idea why. That won't stop folks from guessing, though,

and there are bound to be some wild theories. Feel free to make some up for your players.

Canny PCs may choose to question Hitchins, and any marshal can tell he's up to no good. He'll deny involvement, though, saying he was on the second floor of the hotel in his permanent room. Hank Hitchins is remarkably convincing and will cast off suspicion in the eyes of most townsfolk. It will take a Hard (DC 20) skill check or superb role-playing to make him break in any way unless the PCs have actual proof that can be used against him. Hitchins is a gambler, and handles or diverts any suspicion with practiced ease (normally a Hard DC 20 Wile + WITS check to catch in a lie). Handle this by lying to your players as best as you can when you're telling them what Hank says. Obviously, if you think it would be more fun to have him break and confess, do so when it's cinematically appropriate.

The sheriff (unless he's already been sobered up by the PCs) will issue a warrant for Brig Olaffson instead of holding Hank Hitchins in jail, and Hank will soon be headed off on a normal trip in his freight coach. He'll actually use this opportunity to flee to the camp of the Haqat, where he hopes to find refuge.

One other possibility: if your players don't suspect Hitchins in the least, and he learns the PCs are headed out to arrest him, he may volunteer to come along and help.

He'll claim to feel responsible for not thinking to stop Brig when he ran. In truth, he wants to make sure that Brig's mouth stays closed for good, hopefully by filling the hill folk with lead during a gunfight. Should he come along, Hank's goals are to not be revealed as a murderer and to kill Brig and his family as quickly and thoroughly as possible, so long as he has an excuse for it.

If Hitchins quietly flees to the Haqat instead of accompanying the PCs to find Brig, the PCs may want to track him down. This is covered in Act Two.

Whelkington, human gravedigger: Lvl 1, GRIT 1, DRAW -1, WITS -1, HP 1 (cowpoke), Def 10, MDef 10. No attacks.

Hank Hitchins, human mentalist: Lvl 4, GRIT -1, DRAW 2, WITS 2, HP 21, Def 16, MDef 16. .32-cal pistol +6 (1d6); mentalist trick +6 (signature tricks are marked): *Charm Person, Hypnotism, Silent Illusion, ESP, Sixth Sense.* Wile skill +8.

Brig Olaffson, hill folk miner: Lvl 1, GRIT 4, DRAW 0, WITS 0, HP 14, Def 11, MDef 11. Hatchet +5 melee (1d6+4) or +1 thrown (1d6, range 0).

WHAT COULD GO WRONG?

Hopefully the PCs will jump to the same conclusion that everyone else has, that Brig shot Whelkington to hide a secret. This should send the PCs off after Brig if for no other reason than to claim the bounty on his head. If the PCs aren't interested, the sheriff may directly ask them to help. If they agree, he'll deputize at least one of them.

If the group still isn't interested, you'll skip the part of the adventure in Brig Olaffson's cave. The group will need to seek elsewhere, perhaps Hitchins' office (once it's clear that he's fled) or with the Haqat, for clues to what happened with those bodies.

If the PCs immediately suspect Hitchins and manage to prove his guilt, they can try to force a confession from him. He'll resist, although papers proving his guilt can be found hidden in the Freight office. Hitchins will likely go to the hangman's noose still lying and protesting his non-existent innocence.

ENDING ACT ONE

By the time Act One ends, the PCs should know that dead bodies in town have been disappearing. They should have somewhere to go to track down the cause, hopefully up to the hill folk mine to find and arrest Brig Olaffson, and they should know that Criojo is a bad and highly controlling cattle baron who has it in for Caledonia Roundhill, and who fanatically insists on being obeyed. They'll also know that something bad is happening up at Carcass Creek, but they probably haven't met the Haqat face to face yet.

They may or may not know that Hitchins is responsible for stealing bodies; if not, they will at the end of Act Two.

If they haven't achieved it already, finish Act One by giving the group enough experience to reach 2nd level.

CHAPTER SIXTEEN
ACT TWO

SUMMARY

Brig Olaffson doesn't realize he's wanted for murder; he just thinks a murderer is still trying to kill him. Up in the foothills at the mining camp, his hill folk clan retreat into their mine for protection. PCs following them soon discover that the hill folk have secretly been using zombies to mine for gold faster than normal. If arrested, Brig Olaffson claims innocence and tells the PCs the truth: Hank Hitchins shot and killed the old gravedigger Whelkington. He just saw it happen.

Meanwhile, Hitchins has either come with the PCs to secretly try and silence Olaffson, or he's lit out of town to hide with the shee tribe known as the Haqat. The PCs will know Hitchins is responsible by the time they return to town. The Haqat can be dealt with peacefully if the PCs prefer, but Hitchins won't surrender without a fight.

Act Two ends when Hank Hitchins is dead or in the PCs' custody, and when they know he was secretly hired by Criojo to steal bodies. If the PCs have learned of Hitchins' involvement during Act One, most of Act Two may not occur.

ACT TWO SCENE I OLAF'S MINE

(EASY CHALLENGE)

The trip from Perdition to Olaf's Mine, the home of a local clan of hill folk, is a fairly easy one that takes no more than two hours on horseback. The trail is well established from the hill folk's many trips into town. If the PCs are hot on the trail of Brig Olaffson they'll be able to see fading signs of his passage. In order for the PCs to catch him before he reaches the mine, however, they'll have to leave just minutes after he did, and each PC will have to make a Hard (DC 18) Toughness + DRAW roll. Brig is motivated to push his horse as hard as possible.

Normal hill folk settlements are set up like a small fortress. Olaf's Mine is as well, but no one is manning the locked gate. In order to get into the settlement, PCs can climb the wooden wall with a Hard (DC 18) Wilderness + DRAW check, pick the lock on the iron gate with a Normal (DC 15) Learning + DRAW test, or simply bash the gate down with a Hard (DC 18) Toughness + GRIT check. No one will stop them, although they'll hear a wild animal roaring somewhere inside. There are also several furiously barking dogs, but these are skittish and will not attack the PCs.

Olaf's Mine has a few outbuildings that serve as a bunkhouse, a kitchen and dining hall, an outhouse, a warehouse, a barn, a workshop and tool room, and an ore processing facility. There's also a blacksmith shop. The PCs are welcome to explore these; it's clear that there's no one nearby, and that every hill folk in the clan (about 20) cleared out quickly. All valuables and food have been taken, but horses have been corralled in an area with fresh water and grass.

Once the PCs have a rough idea of how many dwarves are in the clan, ask them to make a Normal (DC 13) Learning + WITS check. A success will reveal that based on what Caledonia Roundhill and other townsfolk mentioned about Olaf's clan, their mining output was more than you'd expect from two dozen dwarves. They must be particularly efficient miners.

The location of the dwarves is quickly apparent when someone walks uphill to the mine entrance. There is a young cave bear chained there to guard the entrance. Although still young, it is huge when compared to most bears, and its roar is ferocious. The bear appears to be chained to the cave entrance by a spiked collar and chain around its neck. Staked into the ground near him is a makeshift sign with a skull and crossbones painted on it, and the words "Stay Out." Apparently the dwarves have retreated to their mines, and they don't want visitors.

WHAT COULD GO WRONG?

If PCs fail every possible skill check and are unable to get past the front gate, encourage creative thinking. Spending several hours piling up rocks to provide a makeshift ramp, or dragging in a dead tree to create an impromptu ladder, will lose the PCs time but eventually give them access to the complex. Should this happen the hill folk will have time to set up one additional deadfall trap down in the mines, as detailed in Act Two Scene 3.

If the PCs completely loot the settlement, they'll have real trouble selling their stolen goods in Perdition. Caledonia won't buy goods once she learns they're stolen. The PCs can sell stolen goods to Hank Hitchins for one quarter their normal value, but chances are they soon won't want to be doing business with him.

ACT TWO SCENE II
THEY HAVE A
CAVE BEAR
(MODERATE CHALLENGE)

This beast is named Snorri. He's an adolescent cave bear in the process of being tamed by Olaf, and he's still vicious. The chain allows him to roam in a one zone area around the front of the cave. If PCs begin to shoot at him, be sure to ask them how close they get. Snorri doesn't retreat into the cave for safety if he is shot. Instead, he roars and strains at the end of his chain with all his strength. After Snorri has been successfully shot once, the PCs have one full round to continue attacking (or running) before Snorri snaps his chain and breaks free. His effort to break his chain will be obvious to anyone viewing him.

Snorri is hairy, scary, and a serious threat even with two rounds of free attacks. The best tactics for fighting him are for PCs to scatter and separate. As Snorri runs after one PC, that character keeps running and finds cover while every other PC shoots at the bear. If Snorri can get both paws and his mouth on one person, they'll probably be calling for the preacher.

Snorri, adolescent trained cave bear: Lvl 3, GRIT 3, DRAW 2, WITS 0, HP 23, Def 15, MDef 13. Claw +5 (1d6+3), with followup claw +5, with followup bite +2 (1d8); or roar attack +3 vs MDef, causes all affected creatures in his or adjacent zones to be automatically trailin' for the next two rounds. Chained at start of combat.

WHAT COULD GO WRONG?

Bad tactics and unlucky rolls could wipe the group out and lead to a very content, well fed cave bear. Remind PCs to use the hill folk outbuildings as shelters should they find themselves outmatched. It's also worth remembering that Snorri won't continue to eat a downed PC until all other threats are removed.

A clever scout may try to attempt to calm Snorri through a rough animal empathy, which would use Wilderness + GRIT or Wilderness +WITS (depending on how they went about it) as a Hard (DC 18) skill check. A shaman may cast *Beast-Talking Spirit* or, if powerful enough, *Calm the Bestial Fury*. Both of these strategies could allow the PCs to circumvent a fight completely.

If the PCs pass Snorri without taking a scratch, congratulate them. They did well.

ACT TWO SCENE III
INTO THE MINE
(HARD CHALLENGE)

Olaf's Mine is unlit and extremely well constructed. Most passages are wide and well supported, with a 6' low and possibly claustrophobic ceiling. Miles of mine tunnels wend out from the entrance and there are a number of possible paths through the labyrinth. The hill folk are currently living in the deepest part of the mine, planning to come back out to the surface in a month or two once trouble has blown over.

There is no tactical map of the mine because a dungeon crawl isn't needed. Instead, focus on the cinematic aspects of exploring a mine. To find out how long it takes to determine the correct route to the dwarves, have one PC roll a Wilderness + DRAW check. It takes a number of hours equal to 25 - the skill check, with a minimum of four hours. If a PC thinks to check for tracks at the mine's entrance, they will succeed with a Normal (DC 15) Wilderness + DRAW check. This immediately reduces the time to the minimum four hours. The PCs can also choose to ride in mine carts, which is more dangerous but reduces their travel time to less than an hour.

There is no reason to dwell on hours spent trudging through the mine unless you want to add some random predators into the dark tunnels. Simply say that the group hits dead end after dead end and gets lost in a tangle of mine shafts and tunnels until they find one tunnel that shows recent signs of tracks.

Olaf and Brig have collapsed several of the tunnels in order to make their refuge more defensible. As a result, there are two choke points that the PCs are forced to go through in order to reach the hill folk sanctuary. These are the mine cart tracks and the Great Span.

ZOMBIE AMBUSH

Instead of putting their own clansmen in danger, the hill folk have taken their six zombies and placed them in key choke points throughout the mine. All are the bodies of former outlaws shot or hanged in Perdition. They have been left behind by the dwarves as protection, told to attack any creature who isn't a hill folk. That means that hill folk PCs will not be targeted directly by zombie attacks, something the PCs may need to figure out on their own.

It is up to you how you want to break these zombies up for maximum effect. A group of 1, 2 and 3 works well; so does three groups of 2 or two groups of 3. The zombies hide in wall niches or ceiling holes and lurch out (and drop down on) the PCs as they pass. Ideally one zombie attacks from the front, and one from the rear, in tunnels or areas where it's difficult for PCs to escape. The zombies can use either mining picks or their normal fists and teeth to attack.

Use these zombies to maximum effectiveness near the mine carts and the Great Span. For instance, PCs riding the mine carts and dealing with unstable tracks may find a zombie dropping down onto the cart from its ceiling perch. Surprise is determined by a Wile + DRAW roll versus an opponent's Mental Defense; a zombie's roll to surprise a PC is usually d20+2. As usual, surprised PCs are trailin' for the first round.

The best way to run this sort of encounter is to give the PCs many methods of defeating the zombies using atypical tactics. For instance, describe a branching track, one of which leads through a high-ceilinged cavern and one of which leads to a cavern entranceway that barely clears the top of the mine carts. If one of the PCs is able to reach down and yank the lever that redirects the track, then everyone announces they duck, you should have one or more zombies instantly decapitated and destroyed. Reward the players' ingenuity and creativity, aim for a cinematic encounter, and give the players multiple chances to shine. In a cinematic game like *Owl Hoot Trail*, saying "Yes and…" works far better than "No."

Zombie, undead outlaw: Lvl 2, GRIT 4, DRAW -1, WITS -4, HP 21, Def 9 (includes penalty for always trailin'), MDef 8. Slam +6 (1d6 +4) or weapon. Zombies are always trailin'. *Undead*.

As each zombie perishes, a wisp of green flame will hang in the air for a second before whooshing towards the southeast and disappearing. This is the demon inhabiting the corpse being drawn back to the shaman who summoned it, but it would take a Hard (DC 20) Learning + WITS skill check to realize this. If the PC fought the Creek demon in Act One Scene 9, they will automatically know it is a demon but not know to where it being drawn.

DEADFALLS

If you wish to soften up the PCs a little, the hill folk have installed up to two deadfalls (or three if the PCs have been delayed in entering the mine, as noted above in Act Two Scene 1.) These traps consist of a trip wire and a collapsing ceiling, and do 2d6 damage to everyone in a one zone radius when they're triggered. A successful Wile + WITS check at DC 15 (or DC 13 after the first deadfall) will spot the loose ceiling rock and the tripwire before it is set off; if the trap is set off, a Normal (DC 15) Toughness + DRAW check will reduce the injury to half damage. It is up to you as to where you place these. Note that hill folk get a +3 bonus to spot underground traps and dangers.

WHAT COULD GO WRONG?

Be aware of pacing while the PCs are inside the mine. Make it long enough to be exciting and interesting, without letting it drag on and become a tedious maze of trap-filled corridors. Getting to the action is the fun part of these scenes.

ACT TWO SCENE IV THE MINE CARTS
(HARD CHALLENGE)

A central hub in the tunnel network holds the beginning of a makeshift mine cart track. The hill folk use these to quickly transport supplies and ore. Riding in these carts is the fastest method of descending down into the mine. If the PCs choose not to actually ride uncontrollably into the darkness in

a cart - and this particular author will be deeply disappointed if they don't - they can follow the tracks on foot.

You are encouraged to use these tracks as a cinematic set piece even if the PCs decide not to ride them, since they lead directly to the hiding hill folk clan. This may involve Hank Hitchins (if he is with the PCs) abandoning the PCs and jumping in a mine cart himself, so as to reach and kill Brig Olaffson before the PCs can; it may involve zombies riding a mine cart down towards the PCs who are walking along the track. As mentioned above, the tracks make a good location for a zombie ambush.

Remember that hill folk get a +3 bonus to spot underground traps and dangers; this bonus applies to noticing and circumventing danger on the mine carts.

Possible cinematic moments with the carts:

* Low ceilings, requiring regular ducking in the midst of a battle.
* Branching tracks, with one set of tracks clearly leading to peril. A Normal (DC 13 or DC 15, depending on how difficult you wish it to be) skill check (usually Toughness + DRAW) will redirect the cart.
* Broken brakes. DC 13 Toughness + GRIT (or perhaps Learning + GRIT if they use book learning to come up with a solution) to slow the cart.
* Separating carts. Mine carts always seem to come apart when racing downhill in tunnels, occasionally traveling briefly on parallel tracks. This may create problems for PCs fighting zombies on separate carts.
* End of the line! Slow the cart (as above) or take 1d10 damage upon impact.

WHAT COULD GO WRONG?

While the mine carts are exciting, remember that they're a means to an end. Avoid putting the PCs in a situation where one missed braking roll results in a total party kill. A better use is to have the carts be an exciting and unusual stage for a gunfight against zombies.

ACT TWO SCENE V THE GREAT SPAN

(MODERATE CHALLENGE)

This vast (5 zones across) natural cavern is the hill folk's last major line of defense.

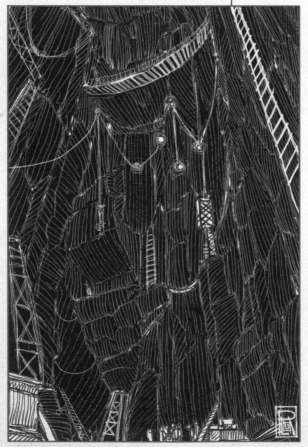

It's hundreds of feet deep, but the hill folk found this cavern to be rich with ore. They have worked this area extensively and both ropes and scaffolding cover the walls and descend from the ceiling. The hill folk have constructed a rope bridge across the cavern.

This area is a good location for a final zombie battle, with zombies dropping from the ceiling or clambering onto the rope bridge. A smarter than average zombie might even try to cut the bridge while the PCs are on it. With a Normal (DC 13) Toughness + DRAW check, give a falling PC ample opportunity to leap onto a rope or section of scaffolding, or cling to the bridge instead of falling to their death.

Olaf Thiggunson, Brig's father and the clan leader, is a hill folk shaman. He waits on the far side of the span out of sight and behind cover. He will wait until as many PCs are in an awkward situation (clinging to the bridge, hanging from ropes in the middle of the cavern) before talking to them. He shouts out that no murderer can come into his mine and assassinate his son, and he'll see all of them dead first. This might catch the PCs' attention.

If Hitchins is with the party he will attempt to kill Olaf before he has a chance to explain the situation. Hitchins will try to make this murder seem reasonable. Hitchins' goal is to keep his secret safe; that certainly involves the death of Brig and Olaf. If it looks like arranging this is impossible, he is likely to flee instead. A gambler knows when to fold if his cards are particularly bad.

If Hitchins is not with the PCs, it's up to them as to how to proceed. Olaf respects strength. A Normal (DC 13) Amity + GRIT check will get him to listen to the true reason the PCs are there. This check is 5 easier if a hill folk is talking, and 5 harder if the PCs are still acting aggressively towards him. Once he understands and believes that the PCs are there to arrest his son for murder and not just assassinate him, Olaf will be enthusiastic to have the truth come out.

The actual miners are not aggressive. They've been willing to let their zombies, traps and trained bear protect them, but they aren't going to ambush or shoot the PCs unless they have no other choice. Remember, as far as they're concerned the PCs are hired killers of Hank Hitchins who have shown up to finish a murder. They're going to be very surprised when they find out that the PCs have a different reason for their expedition into the mine.

Brig Olaffson, hill folk miner: Lvl 1, GRIT 4, DRAW 0, WITS 0, HP 14, Def 11, MDef 11. Hatchet +5 melee (1d6+4) or +1 thrown (1d6, range 0).

Olaf Thiggunson, hill folk shaman and clan leader: Lvl 3, GRIT 2, DRAW 0, WITS 2, HP 20, Def 13, MDef 15. .45-cal revolver +3 (2d6, range 0-2); spirit attack +5 (signature spirit powers are marked): *beast-talking spirit*, *mending spirit*, *calm the bestial fury*, *twisting the wood*.

WHAT COULD GO WRONG?

It's possible the PCs will leave the mine after encountering the zombies but before reaching the hill folk. This means that Hank Hitchins' perfidy won't be uncovered for some time to come. If Hitchins was with the PCs, he'll continue into the mine to try and kill off his witness. If Hitchins has fled to the Haqat, Criojo will soon hear of this and be concerned that his secret collection of zombies is soon to be uncovered. Should that occur, Criojo will put his plan to completely control - or conquer - Perdition into motion.

It's also possible that the PCs will kill all the hill folk without talking to them first. Certainly, this is what Hitchins would prefer. If this happens, you can either have a young hill folk boy surrender and tell them the truth, or you can watch the look on the players' faces later when they learn the truth.

ACT TWO SCENE VI REVELATIONS
(EASY CHALLENGE)

Whether the PCs have made peace with the hill folk or they've slaughtered enough of the clan for the rest to have surrendered, they're going to have questions. Brig will tell his story if he is still alive. Read or paraphrase the following.

"I'd paid to sleep in a nice comfortable bed for a change," Brig endures withering looks of scorn from the other members of his clan, who correctly suspect he'd paid for companionship, "and I was walking down the corridor of the hotel. A shot went off in the room right next to me. I opened the door without even thinking about it, and Hank Hitchins - you know, the man who owns the stagecoach and freight company - was standing with a smoking pistol. Whelkington was lying on the bed, dead as can be. Hitchins saw me, shook his head, and started to raise his gun. I just ran.

I already owe the man some money from gambling debts, I didn't want him to murder me as a witness as well. I figured this was human trouble. Whatever it was, it'd blow over, so I came back here."

The PCs are bound to ask about the zombies. Olaf will look embarrassed but he'll defend himself. "I bought them from the Haqat, that tribe of shee outside of town. Hitchins is the man who told me about them. I figured that they'd been lousy no good murderin' outlaws while they was alive, and we wanted help in the mines. Someone who can dig 24 hours a day for no pay seemed like the way to go."

When everything is straightened out, the friendliness of the hill folk depends on how the PCs treated them. The group may get an escort out of the mine, and Brig might volunteer to come down into town to clear things up; or he might refuse and have to be dragged out. Either way, the PCs will have to promise that Hitchins won't be a threat if they want Brig's and Olaf's cooperation.

ACT TWO SCENE VII FINDING HITCHINS

The sheriff will pay the PCs any reward owed for Brig's capture, even if Brig is known to be innocent. The default is $50 alive, nothing dead.

At this point the PCs likely know that someone has been stealing bodies, that Hank Hitchins killed the gravedigger to cover it up, and that dead bodies are being turned into zombies. If he hasn't already, the sheriff will likely ask for the PCs' help unless they've been more trouble than they're worth. The PCs are likely to want to either find Hitchins or talk to the Haqat. Luckily, unless the PCs have already captured or killed Hitchins,

they're both in the same place. The bounty on Hitchins will be set at roughly $200 alive, $50 dead.

It's likely that the PCs have also put two and two together and have realized that if Criojo had a pocket watch from Caledonia's grandfather, he was buying zombies as well. They may wish to ride out to Victory Ranch and investigate; if they do, use the information in Act Three to decide what happens.

ACT TWO SCENE VIII ENCOUNTERING THE HAQAT
(MODERATE OR DEADLY CHALLENGE)

It may take several days of scouting to track down the exact location of the current Haqat village. The tribe of shee moves around frequently. Placing a watch on the watering hole at Carcass Creek may result in faster success, especially if there are any corpses that the Haqat have not yet animated.

Unless you decide otherwise, the PCs will track down the Haqat at their current camp south of Perdition. The PCs will be intercepted by a group of 12 Haqat on horseback. All the shee are armed, although they do not have their weapons drawn or aimed. The Haqat will ride to intercept the PCs, then sit silently on their horses and wait for the PCs to tell them what they seek. If the party does not threaten violence and is at least moderately polite (ask for a Normal (DC 13) Amity + GRIT check if you think the role-playing is unconvincing), the Haqat warriors will escort them to meet with their shaman Seven Bright Flames. If the PCs threaten violence, the Haqat will order them away.

They'll only attack if the PCs attack first; with 12 warriors, such a conflict is unlikely to end well for the PCs.

As a group, the Haqat give the impression of being silent and implacable. Their faces show little emotion, they stare almost without blinking, and they try to give away little. Amity checks involving these shee are at a -2 penalty unless the Haqat have warmed to the PC for some reason.

The Haqat village has almost 100 shee of all ages living in it. Their corps of warriors is smaller, with approximately 50 male and female shee who are willing to pick up a bow or a gun and ride into combat. They aren't particularly warlike or hostile, however; the PCs will be shown the same level of respect that they have demonstrated towards the shee up to this point.

Hitchins has taken refuge here if you have not decided otherwise. He is relying on Seven Bright Flames to protect and shelter him. Unfortunately, he doesn't realize that the demon consuming Seven Bright Flames' soul has erased much of her empathy, and she is likely to turn him over to the PCs if given a good reason.

The PCs will be escorted to the tent of Seven Bright Flames.

She is sitting outside, cross-legged by a fire. She appears extremely old and her voice is weak. Her eyes are sharp, however, and she watches the PCs carefully as they sit down to talk. Seven Bright Flames is a powerful shaman, and she is prepared to have the PCs beaten and captured if they threaten her with violence. She will ask them about themselves, about what they have been doing, and about why they are here. Her questions are wise and probing.

Seven Bright Flames does not generally lie. If the PCs ask her about zombies, she will

admit that she has created each undead at the sacred spot near Carcass Creek. If asked why (and this is a partial truth), she will say because Alberto Criojo asked for a weapon to use against the town of Perdition. If asked about Criojo, she tells them that the cattle baron has bought dozens of zombies from her over the years. She does not know why, or where he keeps them. It is her impression that he is saving them for some sort of war. She will smile, an ancient toothless smile, and tell the PCs that Perdition will be safer from Criojo if her creations are destroyed. If they ask that she create no more zombies, she laughs, and tells them to destroy the ones she's made already. Then she will consider their request.

What she is not telling the PCs is that the demon inside of her has gotten stronger with every fiend drawn up from Hell and placed within a dead body, and will become stronger still as each of those dead bodies are destroyed by warriors who are not destined for the Pit. The green wisps of flame that the PCs saw while destroying zombies in Olaf's mine (if this has occurred) were these spirits returning to Seven Bright Flames' body. If the PCs eradicate the zombies that the hill folk and Criojo have kept, each of the chained demons are reabsorbed by the shaman's spirit. Seven Bright Flames will die and become something dark and horrible when this happens. No one knows this, although the rogue Haqat Two Red Horses suspects.

If the PCs ask about Hitchins, the shaman confirms that he has run to them for protection. If they demand him they will receive nothing but hostility; if they ask for him politely, Seven Bright Flames looks at them for a minute and assents. Shee warriors drag Hitchins out from his tent, knock him to the ground, bind his hands and feet, and give him to the group. Hitchins will object until gagged.

Once the refugee is handed over, Seven Bright Flames will tell the PCs to leave. If the PCs do not take Hitchins with them when they leave, Seven Bright Flames will eventually have him tortured to death. He may object to the PCs, but he's better off leaving with the group.

Seven Bright Flames, shee shaman: Lvl 5, GRIT -2, DRAW -2, WITS 4, HP 24, Def 13, MDef 19. No weapon attacks; spirit attack +9 (signature spirit powers are marked): *minor flame spirit* (1d6+5 dmg), *spirit veil*, *angering the spirits of iron*, *curse of vermin*, *call forth the dead voice*.

Unnamed Haqat Warrior, shee scout: Lvl 1, GRIT 2, DRAW 1, WITS 1, HP 12, Def 12, MDef 12. Hatchet +3 (1d6+2); long bow +3 or +4 at range 3 or more (1d6+1).

WHAT COULD GO WRONG?

If the PCs try to start a fight with the Haqat in their home village, they will almost certainly be wiped out. Seven Bright Flames is a powerful shaman and there are many Haqat warriors. If the PCs behave with honor, however, they will earn respect that might benefit them later.

The shaman will volunteer information, but it's possible that the PCs may not discover that she has been raising the dead. If so, Hitchins or Two Red Horses can inform the PCs of this.

It's possible that Seven Bright Flames may be killed in this scene. For instance, the PCs may decide that a shaman who reanimates the dead can not be permitted to live and so they sneak back into the Haqat camp to assassinate her. She can not transubstantiate into a demon unless the zombies she created are destroyed, so successfully slaying her earlier will prevent this adventure's Epilogue. If this occurs, be sure to describe the horrific demon attempting and failing to claw its way out of her flesh. You want your players to feel good about their decision, especially since there's probably about to be a village of furious Haqat warriors riding after them.

ACT TWO SCENE IX INTERROGATING HITCHINS

(MODERATE CHALLENGE)

Hitchins is a gambler, and he will bargain for his life with what chips he has left. The mentalist isn't shy about using his powers to great advantage, and will utilize *ESP*, *Sixth Sense*, *Hypnotism* and *Charm Person* to try and flee or talk his way out of any trouble.

Hitchins is an awful person and a mind-influencing huckster, but at heart he's a flunky and he'll rat out his boss if he thinks there is no other way to save his life. Whenever it may occur, use this interrogation to fill in plot holes that the PCs need but haven't yet figured out. Hitchins tries to blame all of these crimes on Alberto Criojo and his obsessive need for control.

This might mean telling everything he knows about working for Criojo:

* acting as an in between for Whelkington and the Haqat

* using his stagecoach to smuggle dead bodies out to the shee

* supplying the Killers of Carcass Creek with supplies

* turning the sheriff into an alcoholic with a fake curse

* how the mayor is under Criojo's thumb

* how Criojo has a barn full of zombies that no one is allowed near

* how he arranged the murder of Caledonia Roundhill's fiancé at Alberto Criojo's request.

He'll even admit to cheating at cards if he thinks it will help. Hitchins doesn't, however, know that Seven Bright Flames is close to becoming a demon made flesh. He just thinks she's going senile.

Hank Hitchins, human mentalist: Lvl 4, GRIT -1, DRAW 2, WITS 2, HP 21, Def 16, MDef 16. .32-cal pistol +6 (1d6); mentalist trick +6 (signature tricks are marked): *Charm Person, Hypnotism, Silent Illusion, ESP, Sixth Sense*. Wile skill +8.

WHAT COULD GO WRONG?

Hitchins is a nice source of information to let the PCs know exactly what is going on, but it's not essential he survive. If he's slain, the sheriff will find papers in his office that hint at the extent of his crimes.

ACT TWO SCENE X THE APPROACH OF TWO RED HORSES

(EASY CHALLENGE)

If you choose to use Two Red Horses as a friend or a source of information, she will be most likely to appear after the PCs have left the Haqat. While she's independent and fierce, she's also badly homesick, miserable that she has forever been banished from the people she loves. Should she and the PCs make friends, it is possible that she'll share her opinion that Seven Bright Flames is not to be trusted. Two Red Horses senses the gnawing evil inside of the shaman, and she hates it. Warning the PCs about the shaman's growing cruelty seems kindest.

If the PCs wish her aid in cleaning up the Haqat shaman's handiwork, Two Red Horses will ride with them for a time. If they don't, she will ride back onto the prairie and watch them from a distance.

Two Red Horses, shee scout: Lvl 2, GRIT 2, DRAW 1, WITS 2, HP 16, Def 13, MDef 14. Hatchet +3 (1d6+2); long bow +3 or +4 at range 3 or more (1d6+1). Wilderness skill +6.

ENDING ACT TWO

If the PCs' actions are varying from the adventure, you're going to see it by the end of Act Two. That's a good thing. By the end of Act Two, Brig Olaffson should be either dead or exonerated and Hank Hitchins should be dead or captured. The PCs should know that Hitchins was working for Criojo and stealing corpses for the Haqat, whose shaman then animated them into zombies and sold them to the hill folk and to Alberto Criojo. They should know that Criojo has been funding some very bad activities in Perdition, and he still has a few dozen undead unaccounted for.

Time for the PCs to visit Alberto Criojo.

CHAPTER SEVENTEEN
ACT THREE

SUMMARY

Act Three centers on the cattle baron Alberto Criojo and the Victory Ranch. As the cattle baron's power base begins to crumble he will squeeze all the harder to gain control, and this means marching a zombie army on Perdition. If he dies, unholy bargains with Seven Bright Flames allow him to spontaneously rise as an intelligent undead at the next dusk. Either way, Criojo's obsessive need for complete control will likely lead to his downfall. Act Three ends with a zombie bloodbath in the defense of Perdition and with the death (or second death) of Alberto Criojo and his bodyguard Steeleye.

ACT THREE SCENE I
CALEDONIA GETS MAD

When the PCs next ride into town, Caledonia greets them and asks what they've found out. She'll gladly feed them food and buy them drinks over at the saloon, and unless they object they'll soon have an audience. The entire town (well, everyone in town not paid off by Criojo, at least) is furious about the desecration of the graveyard. Once the PCs tell their story, Preacher Amanda Cole in particular is calling for Hitchins

and Criojo's necks in a hangman's noose.

This scene is a significant payoff for the players. It's when they get to reveal everything they've uncovered, and the worried townsfolk hail them as heroes for uncovering the crimes. Their appreciation is as much of a reward as a monetary bounty.

If you wish the sheriff to have a heroic story arc, now is when he takes his stand. He'll admit publicly for the first time about how he was drugged with (what he believes is) cursed whiskey. The PCs may have learned the truth from Hitchins; if so, the sheriff will try to get sober for the first time in more than a year. He might actually do it, too, if the PCs or his friends have time to help.

Unless the PCs have a better plan (and they might), the townsfolk are agitating for an 8-man posse to ride out to the Victory Ranch and arrest Criojo. Stealing the dead, stealing *from* the dead, and then having their loved ones raised as zombies? No punishment is too good for him.

WHAT COULD GO WRONG?

The PCs may choose not to head to Criojo's ranch, preferring to let the posse handle it. That's fine; see the next scene for details on how that turns out.

For an easy method of tracking cowpunchers in a large fight, put a penny out for every cowpuncher in the shootout. If they are hit once, flip the penny to show that they are wounded; if they're hit again or injured, remove the penny to show that they are dead.

ACT THREE SCENE II CRIOJO'S RANCH

(HARD CHALLENGE)

The Victory Ranch is a large house, a number of outbuildings, and several large barns (one recently burned). Criojo owns dozens of horses and thousands of steers. When the PCs and their posse approach, however, he has ordered a half dozen cowpokes to watch silently and follow his lead. Criojo's family will be watching in terror from nearby, close enough to plead for his life but far enough away not to be easily caught in a crossfire.

Spies and scouts in Perdition can be an advantage. Previously informed by his remaining informants to expect a posse, Criojo has removed the zombies from his property. He considers himself far too smart to get caught so easily.

As a result, Criojo will meet the PCs' posse at the entrance of his ranch. He has his family, Steeleye, and 6 cowpokes with him. He coldly refuses the posse entry onto his property, stating that they have no cause to be there. When you role-play Criojo, remember that this is a man with icy certainty that he is correct, and utter disdain and fury for anyone who defies him. Criojo doesn't often visibly lose his temper, but when he does it is a terrible thing to behold. He'd probably bullwhip to death someone who defied him, but just like most bullies, he'd want to do so in private. In front of strangers, his manners are ironclad and haughty. If asked where the zombies went, Criojo will only smile thinly and claim that he has no idea what the PCs mean. The truth can't be pried from him with a skill check.

When the PCs and anyone else in the posse gets onto Criojo's ranch, they'll discover that there are no zombies on the ranch at all. No real evidence, either; the barn that Hitchins may have claimed the zombie horde was kept in apparently burned down the night before. Criojo stiffly orders the posse off his property once again since there's no evidence against him. If the sheriff or the PCs try to arrest him, he will order his men to shoot them all down. Criojo, although he'll seek cover, will never raise a hand in violence himself. He's too proud for that. He also won't run. He's no coward. If all his men fall and he's still alive, he'll go with the PCs willingly. He knows that he has a backup plan.

This can be a deadly fight, although the PCs likely have NPC allies with them to help even things out and absorb some bullets. Should Criojo be killed in this fight, a previous ritual with Seven Bright Flames causes him to rise again at midnight as an intelligent undead.

Alberto Criojo, human cattle baron: Lvl 4, GRIT 2, DRAW 1, WITS 1, HP 24, Def 15, MDef 15. Improvised melee weapon +6 (1d8+2). Enraged 1/day for 4 rounds, for +3 atk and dmg but -3 WITS.

Steeleye, hill folk gunslinger: Lvl 4, GRIT 2, DRAW 3, WITS -1, HP 24, Def 17, MDef 13. Throwing knife +6 (1d4+2); two .45-cal revolvers +5/+5 (or only one at +7) (2d6+3, range 0-2 each). For one attack per day (decided whenever you like), gain +2 to hit due to his evil eye.

Criojo's cowboys, human ruffians: Lvl 1, GRIT 2, DRAW 2, WITS -1, HP special (Cowpuncher), Def 13, MDef 10. .32-cal revolver +3 (1d6, range 0-1); dirty fighting +3 (1d6+2). Enraged 1/ day for 1 round, for +3 melee dmg but -3 WITS. As Cowpunchers, these ruffians die after receiving an injury or being hit twice for any amount of damage.

Posse members, human gunslingers: Lvl 1, GRIT 1, DRAW 3, WITS 0, HP special (Cowpuncher), Def 14, MDef 11. .32-cal revolver +3 (1d6+1, range 0-1). As Cowpunchers, these ruffians die after receiving an injury or being hit twice for any amount of damage.

WHAT COULD GO WRONG?

The easiest way to run this fight is to have the posse target Criojo's cowboys and vice versa, with the PCs facing down Criojo and Steeleye (perhaps with a few bullets aimed their way to keep things interesting.) If this happens, only run the PCs' fights and assume that the posse wins with two members left standing.

There are several ways the PCs can approach a confrontation with Criojo. For a cinematic scene, try to steer them towards one that allows Criojo to be cruel to them before the shooting starts. He has no fear of death, and the PCs will hate him that much more.

If the PCs never head to the Victory Ranch to arrest Criojo, the posse and Criojo's men will kill one another. Criojo will be mortally wounded in the fight, just in time to join his zombie invasion as an undead, and Steeleye will survive to plague the PCs at a later date.

ACT THREE SCENE III ZOMBIE TRACKS
(HARD CHALLENGE)

When Criojo dispersed his army of undead and sent them towards Perdition, he divided them into four groups of roughly 10 zombies each. Each group was instructed to hide in the prairie and rocky wastes until nightfall. At dusk, all 40 zombies will invade the town from different directions. Depending on what time the PCs headed out to the Victory Ranch, this may occur before they're returned to town.

PCs can track the shambling undead through the prairie with a Normal (DC 15) Wilderness + DRAW check. Assuming that dusk hasn't yet fallen, the undead will be hidden long before the PCs reach any of the four groups. It's up to you how they're hidden; feel free to go for maximum shock value if possible. Perhaps they've buried themselves in loose soil and lurch upwards, perhaps they are hidden amongst boulders on a rocky hillside and start a small avalanche, or it could be they've immersed themselves in a watering hole. Make their appearance memorable.

Ideally, you want one or more groups of zombies to survive detection long enough to march on the town at nightfall. If the PCs find a group and it is not yet dusk, the undead will start shambling towards Perdition and attacking any PC who attacks them en route. This allows the PCs to hang back on horses, shoot at zombies, and try to maneuver out of their reach. If a zombie group loses 5 zombies (half of their members), they focus on one PC and rush him to try and take him down. Keep the combat fresh and interesting. You don't want the PCs bored, shooting at undead with no risk to themselves until they run out of ammo. If there is a preacher with a *rebuke undead* prayer, try to put him in a position where a killing force of zombies are held at bay only by the power of their prayer. That's a scene they'll remember.

Whenever you are describing zombies, remember that these aren't faceless undead. They are the corpses of the men, women and children of Perdition. Local townsfolk knew and loved these people. Use this for drama, shock and horror as needed. In addition, a cold green wisp of ghostfire hangs for a second as each zombie is destroyed. The fire then quickly disperses towards whatever direction Seven Bright Flames is in. As mentioned previously, the PCs are seeing the demonic spirit returning to the shaman. If the PC fought the Creek demon in Act One Scene 9, they will automatically know the fiery apparition is a demon, but will likely not know to where it is being drawn.

The PCs' posse will likely need to split up if they want to get Criojo back to jail and find the different locations for the hidden zombie horde. If you want to ensure that at least a few zombies survive for a nighttime attack on Perdition, it's easy to have those undead be ones that the NPCs simply missed.

Zombie, undead townsfolk: Lvl 2, GRIT 4, DRAW -1, WITS -4, HP 21, Def 9 (includes penalty for always trailin'), MDef 8. Slam +6 (1d6 +4) or weapon. Zombies are always trailin'. *Undead.*

WHAT COULD GO WRONG?

The PCs may have no interest in tracking zombies. If so, they may well be surprised come nightfall. If the PCs do not return to Perdition that night and do not see burning buildings lighting up the horizon, they will return to a town full of death and undead, with the few remaining survivors hiding in the steeple of a surrounded church.

ACT THREE SCENE IV ZOMBIE SIEGE
(HARD CHALLENGE)

The remainder of Criojo's zombie army will attack Perdition soon after nightfall. Shambling out of the darkness from every direction as the church bell peals out a warning, undead children and parents of Perdition's citizens will attempt to slay and devour every townsfolk they see. The screams of the living are as much of horror as they are of pain. If he remains alive and free, Alberto Criojo will stroll amongst them giving them direction, delighted at long last to punish the weaklings who for so long defied him; if he is undead and free, he will do the same but inspire much more horror in the process.

If the PCs are able to slay the undead Criojo, all remaining zombies have their Def and MDef reduced by 2.

Obviously, having the PCs kill 40 zombies could be an exercise in tedium. Allow your players to chose where in town they want to focus, and concentrate the action there. Do they want to protect Caledonia from inside her General Store? That's where her undead grandpappy will try to throttle her. Do they want to

shoot from the balconies of the saloon as Chet and his undead friends come a-callin'? The zombies will stagger into the bar to devour the piano player, and Chet will come for the PCs.

Focus on an interesting battleground, and let the players show you where they want to make a stand. One excellent location for a zombie siege is the church. Many townsfolk will have taken shelter there with Preacher Amanda Cole, and she will be doing her best to fend off the undead. The effort of casting prayers is slowly killing her, however, and the refugees may not be able to hold out much longer if the PCs don't come to their rescue. Set the building on fire to raise the stakes even higher.

The PCs should fight just enough zombies to make for a challenging, terrifying fight. Any additional zombies will be dispatched by the surviving townsfolk, possibly led by the sheriff if he has been rehabilitated. Encourage the PCs to use unconventional means for warfare. For instance, if you allow the PCs to find dynamite or other black powder explosives, a great many zombies can be taken out at once with one or more very cinematic explosions and fires.

With every zombie killed, a momentary wisp of cold green flame can be seen hanging in the air and then rushing to the southeast, the direction of the Haqat camp. Shamans and preachers may fancy that they see a horrible and contorted face in the flame.

Alberto Criojo, human cattle baron: Lvl 4, GRIT 2, DRAW 1, WITS 1, HP 24, Def 15, MDef 15. Improvised melee weapon +6 (1d8+2). Enraged 1/day for 4 rounds, for +3 atk and dmg but -3 WITS.

Undead Alberto Criojo, zombie terror: Lvl 4, GRIT 3, DRAW -2, WITS 3, HP 25, Def 12, MDef 17, slam +7 (1d8+3). Once per day, one round after being apparently killed he springs back to his feet with 10 hit points. *Hardy 2. Undead.*

Zombie, undead townsfolk: Lvl 2, GRIT 4, DRAW -1, WITS -4, HP 21, Def 9 (includes penalty for always trailin'), MDef 8. Slam +6 (1d6 +4) or weapon. Zombies are always trailin'. *Undead.*

WHAT COULD GO WRONG?

Focus on individual encounters and not on the tactical defense of the entire town unless that's the sort of encounter your players love. If it is, give them a sketch of Perdition and let them plan the town's defense. There's no need to play out the death of each and every zombie. If their plan is a good one, run combat encounters where zombies may be able to sneak through their weaker defenses. So long as they feel like they have earned their victory, and they have the opportunity to once again face the undead Alberto Criojo commanding his zombies, the encounter will be a satisfying one.

ENDING ACT THREE

By the time dawn rises, the last zombies are either slain or hiding in basements ready to prey on the living once again. The town is likely in partial ruins, with buildings burned out and many townsfolk dead from the assault. At the very least, there's a whole lot of bodies that need re-burying in the local cemetery. NPCs such as the sheriff and the preacher may have fallen in (or out

of) love during the siege, and it's a day of celebrating the living and picking up the pieces in a town that's been saved.

A posse will head out to the Victory Ranch and officially place it under the mayor's control. If Mayor Reginald Johnson hasn't survived, pick a new NPC (or even a PC) to serve temporarily in his place. The posse will make sure that there are no more surprises hiding up at the ranch.

There will be some closure. Caledonia will get her grandpappy's body back. The PCs will be given property in town, if they want it. Hill folk gold production will drop precipitously in coming months, now that they're no longer using zombies as miners, but Brig and his clan will personally thank the PCs if it's appropriate to do so. Any other NPCs with a connection to the PCs may say a few private words to them as well.

Once the PCs have had a chance to catch their breath, mourn their dead and do whatever errands they wish, they'll be asked to go speak to Seven Bright Flames in the Haqat settlement. She should be encouraged to never create zombies again.

Before they do so, at the very least the townsfolk will have someone give a quick speech publicly recognizing and thanking the PCs, and Caledonia will give them her grandpappy's pocket watch if she now has it. If they've helped the town, they will always be welcome in Perdition.

If they haven't achieved it already, finish Act Three by giving the group enough experience to reach 3rd level.

CHAPTER EIGHTEEN

EPILOGUE

SUMMARY

In the epilogue, the PCs visit the Haqat to speak with Seven Bright Flames. They find out the shaman fled after slaying dozens of her tribe. Tracking her to Carcass Creek, the PCs confront the transformed shaman once and for all and put an end to her evil.

EPILOGUE SCENE I
THE SMELL
OF DEATH

PCs can smell the fires and the burning before they get anywhere near the Haqat settlement. The typical scouts are nowhere to be seen, and the PCs can approach unchallenged. That alone will warn them that something has occurred.

The Haqat camp is horrifying. Dozens of injured shee writhe in pain, burned and delirious. Dozens more are laid out in long lines, dead. The ground around the shaman's distinctive tent is a charred crater in the earth, and seven sooty lines of char stretch out from the spot into the camp around it. Every tent or object the seven charred lines touched is completely destroyed by fire. A Normal (DC 13) Wilderness + DRAW skill check will reveal that the fire smelled like brimstone,

something they may have last scented up at the watering hole on Carcass Creek.

A shee tribesmember will come talk to them. She is in shock and is exhausted, but will describe what happened. After nightfall, green ghosts of flame began swooping into Seven Bright Flames' tent. First one, then a few, then dozens of them. PCs will immediately recognize these as the same wisps of flame that appeared after each zombie was killed. The shaman staggered outside of her tent, alive with spirits, and she ignored anything that was said to her. It seemed to the shee that the shaman they knew and loved was gone by then, and something terrible was inside of her skin in her place. As each spirit slammed into her, she seemed to grow in height and power, until finally she simply exploded.

The blast and seven arms of cold green hellfire were horrific to behold. Many tribesfolk were instantly killed. What was left of Seven Bright Flames was no longer shee; it was clearly some other creature wearing a shee skin. "The shaman bargained with me for eternal life," it said, "but she was foolish and now she is gone. I walk in her place, and I will make this world *burn.*" And then it simply walked away out into the prairie.

For an easy method of tracking cowpunchers in a large fight, put a penny out for every cowpuncher in the shootout. If they are hit once, flip the penny to show that they are wounded; if they're hit again or injured, remove the penny to show that they are dead.

The shee will accept any aid the PCs can offer, including temporary refuge in Perdition. Despite this, the shee thank the PCs for what they have done in destroying the undead. If you think it appropriate, the tribesmember will offer exceptional horses to the PCs as partial recompense for the Haqat's part in raising undead.

EPILOGUE SCENE II TRACKING SEVEN BRIGHT FLAMES

(EASY CHALLENGE)

No skill check is initially needed to track the fiend that wears Seven Bright Flames' skin. Her footprints are literally burned into the ground. They are headed northeast, and an Easy (DC 10) Wilderness + WITS skill check reveals that they are on a direct course for the boneyard of Carcass Creek. The tracks fade out after a few miles, but their direction never strays. The group will know their destination for miles ahead of time, because the sky around Carcass Creek is bright with cold green ghostfire.

WHAT COULD GO WRONG?

If the PCs choose not to pursue Seven Bright Flames because they are too injured or tired, you have several options. You can have a young shee shaman offer healing, you can extend the amount of time that the demon's ritual needs before it is complete, you can

ignore the ritual completely and have the demon reappear at a later date as a reoccurring enemy, or you can allow the PCs to fail. Choose whichever solution seems like the most fun for your group.

EPILOGUE SCENE III BRINGIN' HELL TO PERDITION

(DEADLY CHALLENGE)

The bones around Carcass Creek have moved from the last time the PCs have been here; every time a zombie was killed, every skeleton around the watering hole was thrown around for a few seconds like a dead leaf in a windstorm. This effect may occur while the PCs are here, if townsfolk are killing off any remaining undead back in Perdition.

The PCs can approach the Creek from any direction they choose. The nameless demon can sense their arrival but is in the midst of a ritual and lets them approach. In fact, they'll soon find out it wants to thank them. Read or paraphrase the following, turning it into a conversation if you can.

"My mortal friends. For generations I have crouched inside of this body, nibbling at the shaman's soul and keeping her from old age. Finally she heeded my whispers to summon cursed souls and create undead. I grew with every corpse, and I grew more when that spirit was returned to me last night. The last shred of her soul remains inside of me, screaming at what she has become. Thank you for all of your help."

Its voice is quite different from Seven Bright Flames'. It speaks whether or not it is being attacked (and the PCs will almost certainly be attempting to interrupt its monologue). By the demon's reasoning, it was the arrival of the PCs that set events in motion and got the zombies killed. It owes them a debt. Sadly, that debt doesn't stop it from attacking them if thcy try to shoot it.

THE RITUAL

The thing that used to be a shaman slowly walks in a ritualistic pattern around the circumference of the watering hole, its feet leaving trails of cold green fire behind it. The network of arcane lines and symbols covers the ground between 2 and 3 zones from the watering hole. For a PC, crossing any number of lines of ghostfire in a round requires a Normal (DC 15) Toughness + DRAW check or suffer 1d4 points of damage. No matter how many lines of fire are crossed, only one skill check and instance of damage is required.

The watering hole roils with cold green light. A Normal (DC 13) Learning + WITS check suggests that the unholy sigils are forcing open a passage straight to Hell. Water from Carcass Creek's watering hole

will temporarily extinguish the burning sigils if poured upon them; other than destroying the demon, there is no other way of disrupting the ritual unless you decide there is.

DEFEATING THE DEMON

The demon must keep up the ritual until midnight. At that time, the pool will open up and the legions of Hell will ride forth. If this occurs, at least you'll have a memorable way to end the adventure.

The monstrosity that used to be Seven Bright Flames is a formidable opponent.

Simply shooting the fiend won't work unless the PCs can do a lot of damage very quickly; the demon regenerates its GRIT in hit points each round, and it can leave the ritual for up to three rounds without the ritual being ruined for the day. This allows it to dart into the next zone with a move + attack (trailin'), attack + move (trailin') back on the second round, and spend its third round continuing the ritual. If the PCs hang back farther than that, the demon can create whirling coils of cold green flame in a range of 1-3.

However, there is a clue to the demon's weakness in the ritual pattern. If it gets within one zone of the water it takes 1d6 damage per round and is in visible pain; if it touches the water it is instantly drawn back down to Hell with its ritual incomplete. The demon recoils whenever it nears the inner edge of the zone. That is why there are no ritual lines near the water and the bones.

If the PCs can lure or tackle the demon into the water they can defeat it without ever firing a shot. This information can be intuited by a Normal (DC 15) Learning + DRAW (for intuition) or Learning +WITS (for religious knowledge) skill check; feel free to provide information or allow other skill checks if the players ask questions.

If the PCs can give the demon an injury, they may be able to move it into the pool before it heals. It will howl in fury and terror if anyone tries this tactic. A brave PC may also be able to move it by closing into melee range and rolling a Hard (DC 17) Toughness + DRAW skill check. It will fight back with everything it has, although making sure to continue the ritual once every three rounds.

Demon of Carcass Creek: Lvl 7, GRIT 5, DRAW 0, WITS 3, HP 38, Def 17, MDef 20. Claw +12 (1d6+5); whirling coils of flame +7 (1d10, range 1-3). Heals 5 HP per round; *Hardy 3* (-3 on all injury checks suffered).

WHAT COULD GO WRONG?

As the final climax, it's now or never for the PCs. They may get frustrated about not being able to significantly hurt the demon. If so, be sure that you've given them enough clues about the demon's movement that they can put two and two together.

It's quite possible that your players will come up with a clever plan entirely different from the solution suggested here. As always, ignore the adventure and go with whatever is coolest.

ENDING THE EPILOGUE

If the demon is defeated and returned to Hell before it completes the ritual, the PCs have truly won. Describe the sound and appearance of the ritual lines being ripped off the ground and plummeting, hissing, into Carcass Creek. The demon will scream and vow eternal vengeance, but they've beaten it for good - unless you decide otherwise.

This act will also close the portal to Hell that lies beneath Carcass Creek. The killing curse will vanish with the demon, and a year from now the area around the watering hole will be alive with the most beautiful wild flowers anyone has ever seen. Someone will hammer in a rough wooden sign naming the spot after the PCs, and life in Perdition will go on.

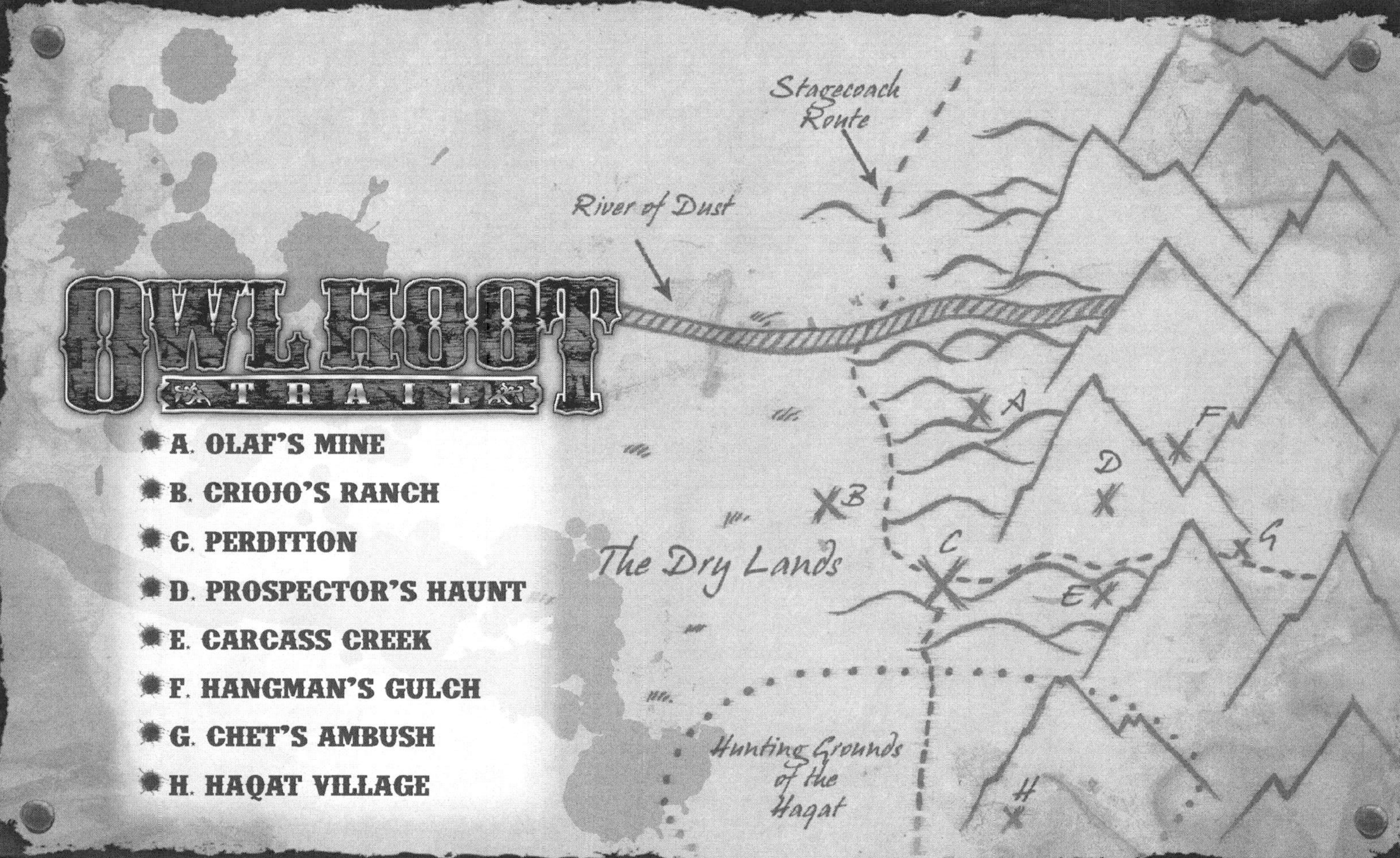

OUTLAW TRAIL

★ A. OLAF'S MINE

★ B. CRIOJO'S RANCH

★ C. PERDITION

★ D. PROSPECTOR'S HAUNT

★ E. CARCASS CREEK

★ F. HANGMAN'S GULCH

★ G. CHET'S AMBUSH

★ H. HAQAT VILLAGE

Stagecoach Route

River of Dust

The Dry Lands

Hunting Grounds of the Haqat

THE TOWN OF PERDITION

A. LAND ASSAYER
B. BANK
C. WAREHOUSE
D. GRAND HOTEL
E. CITY HALL
F. MAYOR'S RESIDENCE
G. EMPTY BUILDING
H. LIVESTOCK MERCHANT
I. GUN SHOP
I. SALOON
K. EMPTY BUILDING
L. BARBER SHOP
M. WOOD SUPPLIES
N. UNDERTAKER
O. STAGE FREIGHT OFFICE
P. MERCANTILE
Q. SHERIFF'S OFFICE
R. THE GALLOWS

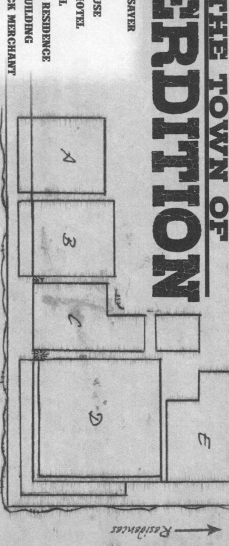

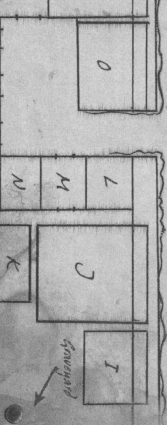

Residences →

← Church & Corral

Graveyard

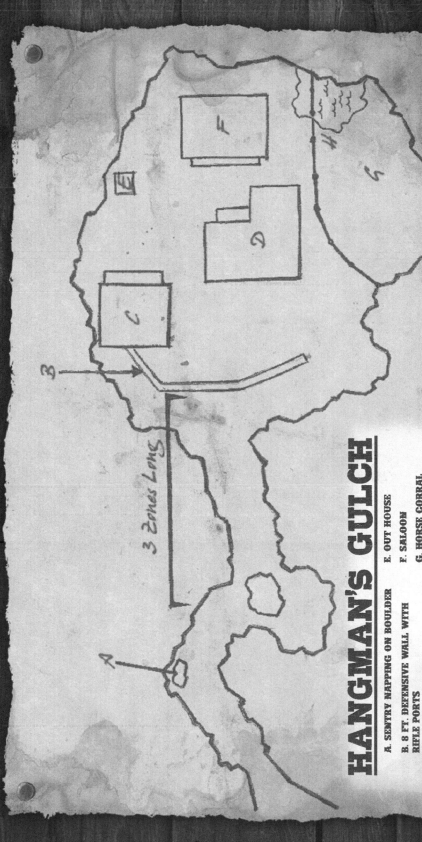

HANGMAN'S GULCH

A. SENTRY NAPPING ON BOULDER

B. 8 FT. DEFENSIVE WALL WITH
RIFLE PORTS

C. BUNKHOUSE

D. MESS HALL

E. OUT HOUSE

F. SALOON

G. HORSE CORRAL

H. WATERING HOLE

3 Zones Long

SKILL USE TABLE

Skill	Examples of Use
Amity + GRIT	Gathering a posse, slowly earning a NPC's respect
Amity + DRAW	Quick-witted banter, making a good first impression
Amity + WITS	Noticing lies, being persuasive
Learning + GRIT	Medical knowledge and practice
Learning + DRAW	Quoting the law, recognizing clues
Learning + WITS	Translation, history, remembering obscure lore
Toughness + GRIT	Climbing, holding up under starvation or torture, blocking a foe from leaving a zone (opposed check)
Toughness + DRAW	Dodging, wrasslin' a steer, bull-rushing a foe into a different zone (opposed check)
Toughness + WITS	Disbelieving mirages, overcoming a persistent effect
Wilderness + GRIT	Crossing a barren desert
Wilderness + DRAW	Hunting a wild animal
Wilderness + WITS	Tracking people, noticing something odd in the wilderness
Wile + GRIT	Intimidation
Wile + DRAW	Most gambling, sneaking (base DC = foe's Mental Defense)
Wile + WITS	Bluffing, cheating when gambling, perception

POWER TABLE

Level of Power	HP Cost	DC for Burnout Roll	Cost to Recharge
1	1d4	14	$5
2	2d4	16	$10
3	2d6	18	$15
4	2d8	20	$20
5	2d10	22	$25

INJURY TABLE

Roll	Effect
2	no effect
3	stunned, lose next action
4	knocked down
5	knocked down & stunned
6	minor injury, knocked out for 2d6 rounds
7	serious injury (broken limb, punctured artery, lodged bullet), 1d6+2 days to heal, *bleeding*
8	major injury (broken ribs, perforated lung, lodged bullet), 2d6+4 days to heal, *bleeding*
9	multiple major injuries or gruesome injury (severed limb, knee shot out), 2d8+6 days to heal, will never be 100% (exact effects up to GM), *bleeding*
10	deadly wound, will die in 3d6 rounds unless bleeding stopped, will likely lose limb
11	fatal wound (gutted, stabbed through the heart, broken neck or back, etc), will die in 2d6 rounds
12+	instant death

OPEN GAME LICENSE